GOD KNOWETH HOW TO DELIVER THE GODLY OUT OF TEMPTATION

11-17-18

To June

GOD KNOWETH HOW TO DELIVER THE GODLY OUT OF TEMPTATION

Mark C. Smith

1603 Capitol Ave., Suite 310 Cheyenne, Wyoming USA 82001
1-888-980-6523 | admin@urlinkpublishing.com

URLink Print and Media is committed to excellence in the publishing industry.

Book design copyright © 2018 by URLink Print and Media. All rights reserved.

Published in the United States of America
ISBN 978-1-64367-085-0 (Paperback)
ISBN 978-1-64367-084-3 (Digital)
Non-Fiction
18.10.18

This book is based on just how true God's Word is since the day that it was establish on the earth, and how God's Word will prevail as truth, and to let the world know, that God's Word will stand true in regarding the 2016 presidential election. Between a man and a woman for president for the United States of America for the first time in America history and how that God will deliver the godly people out of that temptation of a woman being in power over the godly as a president of the United States of America, and how that God will protect his word what is written in The Bible the power-the truth and they that live by that word that teaches us that it is wrong for a woman to be in that much power as a President of the most powerful country in the world at the moment. This book will reveal through numerous of biblical scriptures from the King James version dated 1611. How that God is totally against a woman running for president for this country, and the reason why a woman will be refused to become president of this country by God. It's all about the power that this country has. It's the power of the people, the word and the truth. This book will let the preacher and the church-going folks all over the world know why Mrs. Clinton will be refused by God to win this presidential election of 2016.

CHAPTER I

The Race

On August 3, 2016, I began writing this book on this wise. I am a motor coach operator, by occupation and I was on a trip that took me to the Black mountain North Carolina, for a week, and I had some time off a whole week to the exact. So, while I was sitting around I began to watch the event of the running mates for the presidential election of the year 2016. Now, this is when God inspired me to become very interested in this presidential race for the White House as president because it was between a man and a woman.

So, God inspired me to write about this election and to let the world know that MR Trump will win this election and the reasons why he will win and the reasons why Mrs. Clinton would be losing this race for the White House and the reason are found in the scripture of the King James holy bible -dated 1611. As I sit in my motel room which has a big picture window on the second floor. From the second floor this picture window gives a view of the mountain and as I was viewing the mountain I noticed that it was very foggy on this morning. And I noticed that the fog was trying to rise to the top of the mountain this fog reminded me of the presidential race for the White House. A lot of people's minds will be very foggy about this presidential race because it is between a man and a woman for the first time, in America history. Not just any woman but a well-known strong mind woman who was running against a man who is a novice to the political arena, this is something that has never happened before in this country a woman as a presidential candidate for president of the U.S.A.

My thoughts and writing will be based on my knowledge of God's word and my understanding of it, so I will base my feelings of this election as I follow it from time to time until November 8, 2016 on the word of God and according to my understanding out of the thing which I have read out of the Bible which is to me the book of life.

You know women have striven to rise above the man since the beginning of time in the days of Adam and Eve, God's first creation of mankind. I understand that there is a movement going on called the ERA equal rights amendment for all citizen regardless of sex. It was introduced to Congress in 1923, you see even long before this date of 1923 women has striven to rise above the man and to be equal with the man in jobs here in the U.S.A. Let me say this before I get into the depth of these thoughts that GOD will be revealing unto me about this presidential election until is over Sure there are women presidents out there in some country somewhere they could be doing well, but God is not concerned about those small countries, but he is concerned about the most powerful country in the world and who is president of it. The United States would never have a female president in power here as president and long as this country hold it's face value with God. As for right now on August 3, 2016, I believe we still had a face value with God. But we as U.S. citizens stand in jeopardy with God because of our current administration, who had done something that God is frowning upon right now. I know the female race by gender wants to be in control of the ultimate power rising to the top the very top of the business world as a president of the United States of America. Well I must tell you all men and women boys and girls all over the world this is not going to happen today because God is against the woman being in that much power, I know some readers are already saying that's not right, well according to God's word and what it teaches us I can speak t so boldly, because his word is truth— let me pause for a moment and say this, I have never watched a presidential race so much as I am watching this one even one of my daughter made this statement—daddy why you watching that stuff so much, because a woman is involved and I know that this is against the teachings in the Bible, as a minister I have to stand with the word of God. As I am watching this presidential race I will write about it according to the knowledge that I have of God holy word and as God inspires me so.

CHAPTER 2

The Broken Command

I know that a lot of females what to see this event happen and some men as well. You see it's a moment that is going on call the ERA, it's like they are competing against what God has said for the woman not to do in his holy scripture——THE BROKEN COMMAND—. 8-3-2016-Black Mountain North Carolina — There was a time at the beginning in the days of Adam and Eve Did you know at the time— that they two walks side-by-side as one they were equal they didn't even have an argument they got along perfectly, you see there was a time when man or woman didn't strive against one another, but something happened to change all of that. One day God planted a garden and he put Adam in this God to take care of it and while watching man God realized that all the creatures that he had created had a mate, but Adam had nobody to help him.

In the Bible, the book of Genesis 2:15- God took man and put him into the garden of Eden to dress it and to keep it. Verse 16- God commanded the man saying, of every tree of the garden thou mayest freely eat[these verses are very essential]-but of the tree of knowledge of good and evil, thou shall not eat of it: for in the day thou eatest thereof, thou shalt surely die, verse 18-and the Lord God said it is not good that man should be alone; I will make him a help meet for him.

So God cause Adam to fall into a deep sleep and as he slept:[operation time]-[now we see where doctor get the ideal from putting one to sleep so they can perform an operation]-he took one of his ribs and with that rib God made woman, and God brought her unto Adam the woman, now as time went by Adam wife was in the garden— Genesis 3:1—[now someone might say what in the world does this have to do with the 2016 election, well less traveled a bit into God's word verse—1—. Now the serpent was subtil-[clever-cunning]- than any beast of the field-[Satan chose the best to do his bidding]- which the Lord God has made. And he said to the woman [the serpent speaking -yea. Have God said ye should not eat of every tree of the garden?-2-and the woman said unto the serpent, we might eat of the fruit of the trees of the garden: verse 3—[listen to this] but of the fruit of the tree which in the mist of the garden, God has said, you should not eat of it, neither shall you touch it, lest you die. -Verse-4—. And the serpent said unto the woman, you should not surely die: [check this verse out please]- for God doth know that in the day you eat thereof, then your eyes shall be open, and you shall be as gods knowing good and evil— do you see the point I am getting to. To be as gods. The serpent said to Eve. That's above her husband's that also above the man and every woman—and Eve will receive wisdom knowledge and understanding of good and evil before her husband and with the evil part she will be able to convince her husband to be partaker of the forbidden tree of knowledge of good and evil because now she has smarts—verse 6— and when the woman saw the tree was good for food and that it was pleasant to the eyes, and a tree to be desired and that it was pleasant to the eyes and a tree to make one wise she took of the fruit thereof and did eat. Let me explain explains something about this situation, +God gave a command to Adam and Eve do not touch that tree, and Adam explained this to his wife do not touch the tree that in the mist of the garden stay away from it I don't care how good it looks do not touch it. Here is the main key why God will be rejecting the woman from being president. of the most powerful country in the world of this year of 2016, -verse-5— ye should be a gods more powerful than any man, she was deceived to go far above the man and be just like the gods. for this cause the woman that is running for the office of the president will lose you just watch and see my word will come to pass as truth because I stand on the word of God the BIBLE, the woman will fail.

God is trying to show the world something here in this year's election of 2016, he is allowing one of the most powerful woman in the political arena to run for the office of president of the United States just to prove to the world that his word is alive and will stand— and it is true and he is going to use a novice just to prove to mankind his word will stand true what he [GOD] has stated in the bible— Listen to the penalties that God will put on man and woman. When God found out what was done he was furious with all three of them. Genesis 3:16— unto the woman he said [GOD]—, I will greatly multiply thy sorrow [do you get what God is saying here]—sorrow—you women and men will be very disappointed in this year of 2016 election because you just can't compete against God and win. [cont.] and thy conception; in sorrow, thou shall bring forth children; thy desire shall be to thy husband and he shall rule over thee. WHAT TO RULE OVER -YES-RULE OVER YOU— You see people this curse that God has placed on mankind. Mrs. Clinton has a husband- [Bill Clinton]— if she was president that means she will have the dominion and rule over him and any other man and women in the United States of America. and let me say God knoweth how to deliver the godly out the temptation]. And to rule over man[women] is against God's words so I say God will prevail in this election of 2016—

Genesis 3:3— Neither shall you touch it, lest you die, when Eve disobeyed her equality with man, died and sorrow took his place upon the woman of the world and now the man is above the woman throughout the generation of time. Genesis 2:17 for the day that the eatest thereof thou shall surely die, you see how everything has been changed and you can't unchanged it because God written a law and put it in force this was the very first law and commandment given unto mankind and one of them fail to obey it and that was Eve.

Chapter 3

The Serpent Went To Eve

97 days before the election. Now consider this, why didn't the serpent go to Adam but instead he went to Eve. Let me explain something here Eve was created from man she is the weaker vessel

1Peter 3:7—Likewise ye husband, dwell with them according to knowledge given honor unto the wife, as the weaker vessel, you mean to tell me that some of the people in this country are trying to put someone that God is considering to be weak in the White House as a president that the Bible classifies as weak. All because you want to make history. Well, let me inform you God will take control of this election with just 97 days left until the election time.

It appears to me that God was putting man and woman on a trial basis. Someone may say how so. Let me explain— God told Adam about the tree in the garden Adam told Eve about the tree in the garden. Now the question is who will be the first one to disobey God's command of the do not touch rule. Will it be the man, or will it be the woman well Mrs. Eve gave in to temptation and killed it for all the women in this country to be equal with the man. Disobedience has consequences you obey you will be blessed, you disobey you will be cursed the curse is now that the woman is put under the man and he shall rule over you I understand that Mrs. Clinton hasn't got a chance to win this election to be a president because God is in control, just watch and see God's word come to pass and victory will be God's word coming to pass on November 8, 2016

There is one thing that I understand, which is, the earth is the Lord he created it is His. Everything belongeth to God. Psalms chapter 24-verse-KJV-The earth is the Lord's and the fulness thereof; the world and they that dwell therein. -verse-2-for he hath founded it upon the seas and establish it upon the floods. You see the Bible states that the earth is the Lord He is the one that creates it and that includes you and me -And it is impossible for God to lie] Hebrews -6:18 That by two immutable things, in which it was impossible for God lie, we might have a strong consolation, who is fled for refuge to lay hold upon the hope set before us. And I am laying hold onto God word because it will stand forever as true.

Now let me say this I am not against the woman if the women stay within the guideline of righteousness and when they step outside of the scripture I must plea God cast.

I think that there are some very intelligent and very smart and good women in this world. Who has strong minds, but their bodies are weak said the Scriptures. Eve couldn't resist the temptation, because she was the weaker vessel. So now we stand here today with the situation that the people of some want a female president for the United States of America but my God says no and it is also stated in his word that teaches me that he will refuse her request and the people which are of the Democratic Party and also some of the Republican Party who is switching from one side to the other.

This desire that the Democrats wants is just too much power to give to the female the woman— King Lemuel mother taught him this Proverbs-definition—a short pithy[expressive]-saying in general use stating a general truth or piece of advice]— [Proverbs 31:3 give not the strength unto the woman, nor the way to that which destroys kings. But there are men and women out there in this country want to do the opposite of what God has stated in his word [GOD] God ruled within the kingdoms of men. in the book of Daniel 4:17-This matter is by the decree of the watchers; [that you]-and the demands by the word of the holy ones[the minister] to the intent that the living made know that the most High ruleth in the kingdom of men, and giveth it to whomsoever he will, and setteth up over it the fastest of men [you see God say the fastest of men and not women] do we not know that some women can be fool or tricked just as EVE has stated in her confession to God-[bastest]you will not be able to control this president he will be to you as an arrogant hard to deal with man to some but God chose Him because God knows what spirit he possesses.

Genesis 3:13— and the Lord God said unto the woman, what is this that he has done? And the woman said the serpent beguiled me [trick or-fool]-and I did eat. Do we see and get the picture I am writing this book on the documentation of the 2016 presidential election between Mr. Trump and Mrs. Clinton to let all the world know that God word said the woman is the weaker vessel you see what confession Eve made to God the serpent beguiled me[the weaker vessel] God will not let a woman by gender in the most powerful position in the world as president because God cannot trust women with that much power or responsibility in whom he God has control. Why can't the woman just be humble and respect God's wishes you're not supposed to have the rulership over the man. Do you not know God resisted the proud but he God gives us grace unto the humble?

James 4:6–But he giveth more grace. Wherefore he saith, God resisteth the proud but he giveth grace unto the humble.

The push for a woman to become president, come from weak minded men and weak minded women that do not understand God nor what his word say in concerning what the Holy Bible teaches and when people do those things that displease God it will cause God to distance himself away from a people that are disobedient to his word just as he did to Adam and Eve. God knew which way to people of the United States of the Democratic Party was going to vote and whom they were going to vote for also. But I know that God will protect his word.

1 Peter 1:25- But the word of the Lord endureth forever. And this is the word which by the gospel is preached unto you— the grass withereth, the flowers fade if: but the word of the Lord shall stand forever [do we get that God's Words will stand forever.

God would have to intervene in this year's election because he can't trust a man. To do the right thing I believe if a woman was in that much power the only one that can lead her is the devil himself.

15

If God word said he ruleth in the kingdom of men, then who will be ruling in the kingdom of women. I know some might say this writer has got it in for the women no-no the truth has to be told and expounded on-I know this country has got its first black man for president and the movement now is saying we need to further this movement of equal rights and now it is time for us as the people of this country give the woman a chance to be president. Well God gave Eve a chance, but she fails and blows her chance with God.

We got very smart business minded women in this country no doubt, but the White House is somewhat of a sacred ground or a hallowed place and it is just forbidden for the female to ruled there. History won't be made in this year presidential election of 2016 between Mr. Trump and Mrs. Clinton because God is very much involved in this country. My hope is that God will be done in this year of 2016 election for president of the United States of America I believe in God and in his word and I know that his word is true because I am a watcher and I know that God word is true. It appears man just don't care what anyone said we are going to put a woman in the White House as president they say. Well, I say you can't stand on a lie because it is false it will let you down, some men and females need to stop trying to prove God's word is wrong and it doesn't mean what it said about women ruling over the man. where are the wise preachers today who understands this election that they may inform their congregation and member about the women being in total control of the most powerful office in this world as of now The United States of America and its military as a president of it?

I know the women have been striving for years to get to the top of the business world as bosses and leader at the top of some corporation trying to reach the top of the mountain like the morning fog when the sun is shining so bright, but the word of God is also shining and its already at the top the very top [HEAVEN]. so, I will like to encourage all people do not try to override Gods word because it settles in heaven.

Men and women boy and girl no one are exempt from being under the word of God. God has concluded all under the penalty of sin that was committed on that day at the beginning of time with

Adam and Eve. Galatians 3:22-But the scripture hath concluded all under sin, that the promise by faith of Jesus Christ might be given to them that believe.

This is just one of the many reasons why God has inspired me to write about this 2016 presidential election because someone needs some answer about some un answer question about why Mrs. Clinton will lose even Mrs. Clinton herself will need the answer why she has lost the 2016 election for president-in whom she was convince that she will be the winner— the answer is in the Word of God.

Just maybe I can help someone out there in this world to understand why Mrs. Clinton will not make it to the White House as the first woman to succeed there as president. Once she has loss I just hope she will realize or come to understand that a curse was put on the woman long before or years before she was born with Adam and Eve and that curse is still active as of this day thy desires shall be unto thy husband and He shall rule over thee I know that the women feel as though they can do a better job than the man as president of this country the U.S.A. -I am not saying that they can't there are some very intelligent women as I have said in our country and I will even say that Mrs. Clinton has the skill that is needed for that job as president, but I must stand with the word of God and God said request denied. [I will be pleading God case].

CHAPTER 4

Changes

God do not want the woman in that position [by gender]. God has commanded the man to have the rule over you and not you are having the rule over him this was the judgement that was past when EVE—ADAM's wife disobey [Genesis 3:16 -And thy desire shall be unto thy husband and he shall rule over thee. do we not understand that God fill both heaven and the earth and He knows everything? Jeremiah 23:24-can any hide himself in a secret place that I do not see him? Do not I fill heaven and earth? Saith the Lord —-when Eve the first female woman that was created disobey God's commandment by eating of the forbidden tree, God stated that the day you eat thereof you share surely the-Genesis 2:17 God said you shall surely die— let's study that phase just a little bit[die] stop living or existing or you won't be able to do a certain thing such as walking on the same level as her husband, do we know that the husband is considered to be the head or strength— those same opportunities are now gone man will now rule for what you because the woman Eve disobedience has killed all that equals forever just study time for a moment and see what answer you come up with has any woman ever been in total power of the most powerful country at any time since this judgment has been passed on all of mankind from God has any woman ever made it to the White House as president or vice president of the U. S.A. as God will not even allow the female to get that close to that office as vice president look at the times it has never happened we are living in the time of the year of 2016 a woman has never made it as vice president all those chances has died with the judgment that God has passed on mankind so you see death is taken hold in a many ways-Mrs. Eve killed it for all woman as of today we see women are not permitted by God to be president of the most powerful country in the world sure you may run for the position but you will not reach that goal for the position although you might have the qualification.

Father time has proven that to us time and time again sure there were 12 women who ran for president before Hillary dated back to the year of 1872—145 years women has tried for that position and fail you see God words will stand forever you know only two women have made it close to the vice president but failure took us to place, do we not think it's very strange that a female has not even been chosen even for the vice president of this country do we get the point as my dad Mr. Mo Smith would say] God will protect his word that's why I can trust what the Holy Bible says from Genesis unto revelation the whole book. I know the women want that equality back it died when Eve disobeyed when God said unto the women and a man you share surely die guess what? A lot of things die, and we just do not have some of the freedom anymore because God does not play this judgment is perpetual forever now you will see one of the sorrows come to pass on November 8, 2016, concerning the 2016 election and I know God's eyes are on this country because of the power that this country has.

Just look at this world today and the way things are changing the women mindset is that they want to do everything that the men are doing these days men go to the battlefield to fight the women don't want to be nurses they want to go to the same battlefield and do likewise fight they want to be on the battlefield as soldier fighting in combat-what!—say this not so. Yes, they want to fight men.

Men play sports guess what the women want to play the same sport[change]-you see the women are basically doing everything that the man is doing these days. Just maybe the women think God is asleep well let me inform you that God is not asleep and so many people will find out just how sleep God is when Mr. Trump whom

God has chosen to wins the 2016 presidential election and move into the White House as the 45TH president of the united states of America and for the women I will say your desire shall fail because God's Word will stand.

CHAPTER 5

God Is Not Pleased

The point that I am striving to get the world to see is that God is not happy with the women trying to rule over man as a ruler or President because God has got saint living in this country and another country as well all over this world there are saints of God that why has inspired me to name the title of this book—God knows how to deliver the godly out of temptation-base on biblical teaches out of the KING JAMES BIBLE dated 1611.

2PETER 2:9—The Lord knows how to deliver the Godly out of temptation, and to reserve the unjust unto the day of judgment to be punished.

A lot of people don't see nothing wrong with a woman ruling as president in this country because they do not know the biblical scripture that are written down for our learning that say that the women shouldn't rule over man and some men as well don't understand these scripture that are written in the bible that we as people might be pleasing unto God our creator because it is spiritually wrong for a woman to rule over the godly people with the power that this country or any other people may I say and there just a lot of church people who just don't understand this –so this why God is allowing me to write about this election that you unknowledgeable folks might understand.

From the beginning woman was only created to be a help meet for the man and not help make trouble for the man but to help him-

Genesis 2:18 -And the Lord God said, it is not good for man to be alone; I will make him a help**meet for him**[to fulfill to satisfy a need or requirement or condition]to help the man and not help make trouble for him. Can you imagine how Adam felt when God pass judgment on Eve his wife for touching the forbidden tree do we think she felt the same way?

I am looking forward toward the days just to see how God will take control of this 2016 presidential election because his word stands in jeopardy by foolish minded people who is so willing to override God's laws and the odds are looking bad for Mr. Trump right now God love to work wonder when the odds are looking bad for that person whom he has chosen for particular job or position.

August 4, 2016. 96 days left until election day—People and the media are stating that Mr. Trump hasn't got a chance—— the odds just seem too bad for him at the moment all I see about these odds is the handy work of God because my understanding of God is that just the way he[God] works at time that when Mr. Trump wins this election people will be so amaze, that my God the creator of the great universe that we live in and just watch God's word unfold in total victory for Mr. Trump, I base everything that I am writing on the Word of God in which I stand and believe that HIS word is nothing but the gospel truth and MR TRUMP will win this year president election over his opponent Mrs. Clinton. The Bible I know that I can depend on it you can depend on it everyone can depend on it if you are in a certain position and you just don't know what to do such as this 2016 president election between a man and a woman all you need is just a little bit of faith in God word the holy bible-God word can be such a lamp[light] unto anybody who is confuse about something such as this 2016 year presidential race and people cannot tell me that they don't have their doubt about whom to vote for the man, or the woman but my God said in his word men are to rule and in this country it all about the POWER, YES THE POWER THAT THIS COUNTRY HAVE -that Mrs. Clinton will lose this year presidential election.

Psalms 119:105—Thy word is a lamp[light]-unto my feet, and a light unto my path- [meaning]—when a person mind is so cloudy or confused about a thing or you just don't understand a situation that you can't see clearly your way God word will light up your understanding or manifest to you the godly way to do the right thing that the lamp that King David was talking about God's Words. You use a flashlight when it is dark so that you won't stumble or there might be something that you just can't comprehend God word will light up that path or unclear thought that one might have and that darkness will flee because the power that the light has and God's Word is light and in him is no darkness at all no unclear thoughts just a clear mind like I have about this year of 2016 election for president -Mr. Trump will win and Mrs. Clinton will lose -because God's word is a lamp and has lightened my path of understanding that Mrs. Clinton will lose the 2016 election and when a person trusts in God word that dark path or lack of understanding will displace— then your mind will be of a clearer understanding—I know that the women are climbing the ladder of success in America corporate office today but I got to say that as far as God will allow the women to go -The top office as a president the female in America will be denied by God because of the present power that it holds and I just can't express this enough.

Because the White House is off limit to the female by gender to rule there as a president of America. God is saying to the women leave that position alone according to biblical scripture it is off limit to the women to be president there sure you can hold some type job there at the White House but not as commanding chief. I am admonishing the women to leave that position alone it is off limit for the women to rule there as president because women your mother Eve broke the equality that she had with God and man her husband Adam and sorry took it to place upon Eve.

The woman is the very first one of God creation that He created on the earth to displease beside the serpent in the act of touching the forbidden tree in the garden of Eden which God commanded them if you touch that tree that is in the mist of the garden ye shall surely die-[I just can't say this phrase enough]- and guess what Eve touch that tree and some of her freedom die and sorrow has taken its place and now the man will rule over you and this is what I come to realize in this year presidential between Mr. Trump and Mrs. Clinton there is no way that God will allow Mrs. Clinton to rule as president in this country the United States -for one his Word-#2 The POWER that this country hold-This country is known for its power and it military strength that it holds as of now and it just impossible for a woman to be president of the United States Of America according to my understanding of God's word-it all about God, the Word, the power, and the truth about his Word-even if it wasn't the most powerful spot in the world it is still wrong for a woman to rule over the man according to what the Bible teaches.

1Timothy 2:12 -But I suffer not a woman to teach, nor to usurp authority over the man, but to be in silence-verse 13—for Adam was form first, then Eve.

1Timothy 2:14-And Adam was not deceived, but the woman being deceived was in the transgression. -Eve obtain wisdom first and knowledge first how to do good and then how to do evil and with that wisdom she attain from the forbidden tree in the midst of the garden of Eden that she ate of, she receive smarts, cunning of words and it gave her power over her husband Adam and with that power she was able to persuade him to be partaker of the forbidden tree which God had said not to touch.

Look what happens when Eve disobey[this all have to do with this 2016 election]—why Mrs. Clinton will lose the election]- She was persuaded to go far beyond her husband and was deceived that she could be a God and this act displease God greatly and it cause God to punish the mother of all females from obtaining the total power over the man.

Now I know some woman in this country as well all this world wants to excel even to the point of being in control of the men in this world and especially in the U.S. as president of its, but god says no!

CHAPTER 6

Reaching The Top

It seem as though some of the women are saying and thinking we woman are tie of being bind up that we woman can't make it to the top office as president let me explain something for our learning as a minister of God I must say this world belongs to God and there are DO'S AND DON'T put in place by God almighty and since God took his word and created us all by saying let us make man in our image after our likeness; Genesis 1:26- 26-So we see that this WORD the same word that created us all and everything else in this world now we as people who was created by our creator which is none other than God we are subject unto him man and women to obey all of his commandments the do's and they don't that are written in the bible and to the women you do have some do's and don'ts that God has put in place and made it a law. . now women if you want to help the man stand with him and beside him.

AND one of the don't is that a woman shall obey her husband and he shall rule over thee Genesis 3:16–Your desires shall be unto your husband-now men what your penalties is you got to work and sweat until water just run off of your face you got to till the ground is what God told Adam now women if you want to be a help to the man stand behind him and help him and not trying to rule over him and putting him down because God has said your desire shall be unto your husband the man.

Now women it is not in the plan of God for you to rule as a ruler or king or a president in the most powerful country in the world as of now the United States of America. I know that the polls once again is looking good for the democratic party at this moment this only proves how many people that have read their bible or even go to church and has a teaching priest to give.

There congregation the correct understanding of the will of the Lord concerning the women ruling over the man.

As God spoke to Moses on one occasion when Moses as God a question who shall I say unto thy people have sent me Moses unto them-Exodus 3:14 -And God said unto Moses, I AM THAT I AM: and he said, thus shalt thou say unto them I AM hath sent me unto you and may I say the same thing THE GREAT I AM HAS-inspire me to write about the truth of his holy word concerning this 2016 presidential election in which he God is against the woman who is trying to succeed there as a president because of his word and the power that this office holds at the moment in this country the United States of America this book is to let the world know the spiritual reason why Mrs. Clinton will be losing this election God word teaches and explain that it is spiritually wrong—for any woman to try to rule over the man and I must say thru out this book that it all about God's Word and the power that this country holds and it wrong for the women try to take the steering wheel and lead this country.

God see these odds and is very aware of the polls and what story they the poll are telling just to prove to the world that He is the GREAT I AM, yes, the world, people all over the world because they are watching this 2016 presidential election between Mr. Trump and Mrs. Clinton with a magnifying glass; because somebody out there know what GOD word has stated about the women ruling over the man as a president and the world want to know will God stand up for his people and protect the godly from this temptation that trying to come our way and God will protect what is written down in the Holy Bible.

Do anyone think that God word will turn unto him void? God's Word will be accomplished in this year 2016 election. Anyone think that the Bible teaching is all a lie about what God's Word has said about the women desires shall be unto her husband and he shall rule over you do people think that this scripture has nothing to do with this presidential election between Mr. Trump and Mrs. Clinton, some may say that this writer has gone mad and don't know what he writes about that's just one opinion but when November 8th, 2016 come and Mr. Trump has won the election will one believe then or not. But God has said that his word shall not return unto him void.

ISAIAH 55:10—So shall my word goeth out of my mouth it shall not return unto me void but accomplish what I please and it shall prosper in the thing which I sent it. God said it will it prosper and that means if I the writer is speaking for God on God behave pleading God cast about what his word is saying about the men and women trying to override God command and laws and try to put a woman in the White House as a president then I know that what I am writing about and the title that God knows how to deliver the godly out of temptation then it will come to pass-you see the book of life(BIBLE)-has spoken once again.

Which is none other than God's Word which was left on record for us to follow and obey every day.

So how in the world is Mrs. Clinton is going to get pass God word and win this election as president when God makes a statement like that and when she loses on November the 8th 2016 will anyone believe me about all that I have written about God word and our creator.

CHAPTER 7

Making Bad Choices

I believe that Senator McCain would have won the 2008 president election if he had chosen a man for his vice president instead of a women, nothing against Sarah Palin, I may say but I must say that God doesn't even want a woman that close to that office as a vice president, do we get the point as my dad would say [bad choices]-isn't that something to take in consideration——I believe that just too much power for a woman to have even as a vice president [remember Eve]—she, Eve wanted the ultimate power——total power and that was Eve mistake and it was her downfall. -so, I will say that was senator McCain downfall and that was his shortcoming of not understanding what the word of God says about the women ruling over the man even as a vice president God says no. You will mess yourself up when you don't know I blame the teacher and some preacher who just don't teach the truth about God's Word concerning the woman ruling over the man in this high position in this world as a president and such as the United States of America a country with a lot of power and let me say amen.

God is very concern who is in charge and running the top office as president of the United States of America God chosen land. If people are not careful they will find themselves fighting against God and his will.

There are a lot of churches in the world today of all kinds of denomination and because of their lack of understanding of God word these many denomination the women are now seeking for position as priest pastor and deaconess which is leadership in the churches in which these position would put the women over the men in the church as their leader, women have succeeded to the pulpit in these churches and yes this subject do have to do with the 2016 presidential election and it is very important to know, that the world may know what the Bible has to say and why the women are being refused to become a president in America and why Mrs. Clinton will be denied and she will lose this presidential race for the white house as the 45th President of the United States of America.

When a female pastor hold a pastor position in a church and she has a husband who is a member and is sitting in the audience she then become his leader and all of the church member leader also this act is against the will of God because He do not except women preacher in all of his churches I know the women feel as though they can do a better job at preaching than some men some women can carry a good sermon and message than some men preacher but disobedience is not a pretty thing to God.

1 Samuel 15:22-Hath the Lord as great delight in burnt offering and sacrifices, as in obeying the voice of the Lord? Behold to obey is better than sacrifice, and to hearken than the fat of rams [Explanation]—so, in other words the woman is saying the man preacher or minister are not doing a good of enough job so we the women are going to sacrifice to sacrifice what God has said other words we the women preacher are going to put aside what God has commanded us to do –and override God's Words and preach anyway and do it our way and preach—we want to preach to the women are saying.

Well someone may ask what is preaching—preaching is none other than telling the truth about God word; if ye women can't obey the truth of God word how in the world can the women preach the truth—if you start out being disobedience all of you followers will be disobedience right alone with you I can say this without carefulness on this subject-God does not except women preacher as pastor in his churches; neither does he recognize it as his church with a woman as it pastor—is anyone mad yet—good may I say this is a wakeup call to the world and this is not a new message this message has been preaching on for years but ears have been dull of hearing and if God does not want the women to be preacher in his churches what make us think that he will accept the women as a president his country that has power like America.

Study your bible and don't study to be nutty it appears to me that men and women of some just don't take God's Words serious enough well may I say being disobedience is not a pretty thing to God and that why Mrs. Clinton will be refused to become the 45th president of America and Mr. Trump will win the election for president of America—God will reverence his word what is written the bible and the truth of his word will be marching on for victory for the man God has chosen-this novice Mr. Trump to win the White House as president of the United States of America all because there is disobedience among many of American who are trying to put a woman in power as a president in this country and this act is displeasing to God people just don't seem as though they are taking God serious enough and they are sacrificing obedience[we going to do it our way]— for disobedience and this will be the democrat down fall also—God word is perpetual—it doesn't change and I won't change either and that why I can trust and stand on the promises of God in which I firmly believe because God word never fail—and because his word won't fail Mrs. Clinton will fail at this position that she is seeking for so diligently.

CHAPTER 8

The Power

Women keeping silence in the churches— all this documentation that I am putting down in writing is for the world learning it is to make one wise to things they don't understand about God such as voting for a woman to be president whom God is totally against because of what Eve the first woman did reaching for that ultimate power to be as God.

This 2016 president election is a situation that most of the American voter just don't understand or they just don't care they the people just want to make history the first woman president of America and that will be history—Most of all of this novel that I the novice writer is about the woman striving to get to certain places where God does not want them to be —ruler or Kings or presidents or preacher or as the Pastor of some church.

If God doesn't want the women to be leader or pastor in the church –what makes the women and men believe that God will allow the women to be president of the most powerful country in the world as of now in which he has the control of –when people don't understand what the will of GOD is or they have been taught the word of life out of the bible they the people will the follow their fleshly minds.

In the book of Proverbs 14:22–There is a way which seemeth right unto a man, but the end thereof are the ways of death-Mrs. Eve thought it was okay to touch and eat of the forbidden tree[WOMEN

THE WHITE HOUSE AS PRESIDENT IS A FORBIDDEN TREE TO THE WOMEN AND GOD WON'T LET YOU TOUCH IT AS A PRESIDENT]——but it only brought death to the world and her [eve] thinking was wrong, and it got her in trouble with her boos and that boss was God our creator and she was fire.

So now we see that the women and men think it okay to run for president of GOD Canaan land call America-I will say lean not unto your own understanding America trust in God on this election and you won't be disappointed on November 8th, 2016.

Proverbs 3:5-7-Trust in the Lord with all thine heart; and lean not unto thine own understanding. In all thy ways acknowledge him, and he shall direct thy paths. Be not wise in thine own eyes: fear the Lord and depart from evil- [it is an evil thing to vote for a woman to be president of the most powerful country in the world and I just can't make this statement enough threw out this book. It's all about God's word and the power]

You see what Solomon is teaching here in this scripture your fleshly mind [yes you]—can tell you to go after things that are not pleasing to God such as voting for a woman to be president for a country.

Just like Mrs. Clinton is going after a job she will never be able to obtain or secure that office as the 45th president of America there is utterly a fault among the democratic voter and Mrs. Clinton maybe her faith didn't inform her that it is wrong for a woman according to the Bible teaching to run for the office as president of America I do not know—but I do know she been wanting that job for some time now but I must say that it is against the laws of God that are written in the bible because of the power that this country has as of right now and God has got a law in place that said the woman shall not rule over the man and that is a law that still in effect in the year of 2016 that dated back to the beginning of Adam and Eve.

May I say once again there is no women pastor in God churches sure in the world churches there is a lot of women pastor and preacher. [explaining the difference]—God's churches hold a life of high standard of godly living, which we believe in living for God daily every day of the week no ungodly deeds being committed staying away from all sinful activity and worldly lust of the flesh, the world churches-live an worldly lifestyle basically do anything they want to do according to their fleshly desire and then go to church on Sunday and sing nearer my God to thee not realizing that God don't even recognize there praise— so there are two type of churches in this world— The Church of God which are the godly church and the worldly church these two are totally different from one another I would that we all speak the same thing and so does God.

1Corinthians 1:10—Now I beseech you, [to plead with or beg]-brethren by the name of our Lord Jesus Christ, that ye all speak the same thing, and that there be no division among you; but that you be perfectly joined together in the same mind and in the same judgment.

You see God's Word has spoken again God church was establish first and yes this also have to do with the 2016 Presidential election. God want me to give an understanding of what his word teaches out of the bible about the women ruling over the man because there is a division in this country with religious belief that is taught out of the world's churches who allow women as leaders-[pastor- priest- minister]- of their churches, that believe they the women have just as much right to the pulpit as the man.

When a woman becomes a Pastor at some church she is that church leader she overseer the spiritual affairs [PREACHER]—of the church she has a husband either sitting at home or sitting in the congregation as a member of her church she the pastor is then become over her husband as a ruler then she the woman pastor is in disobedience to the laws of God. God forbids.

Now on the other hand if a church has a man—as its Pastor and he has a wife that sits beside him not as an assistant pastor but as his wife is a help meet—[remember Eve] then she is able to speak in his stead at time because she is being a helpmeet to him as being one with him the man her husband.

From these admonishments that I have just written is to let you know that from the church to the highest office in this country as a president the women with be rejected by God Almighty to become a ruler or a president of America so therefore Mrs. Clinton will lose the 2016 presidential election and I will stand on the word of god whom he will protect his word and what it has stated and this is a bold statement.

This country, America, is a country that has moral that the other country around the world don't have— this country has value— this country has power that the other country does not have this country shows love for its fellow man and its neighbors and all over the world the United States of America has shown love for their fellow man this country started out with godly fear and respect toward God our creator this country believe in freedom and that's why the Pilgrim left England to be free to worship God freely and God lead the Pilgrims across the seas to this great land that I call GODS Canaan land AMERICA—flowing with milk and honey—other word flowing with all kinds of blessing and resources of all kind so you can survive and make here in America.

AMERICA—It's a land that calls the land of the free so by these few things which I have just mention God has bless us.

AMERICA—God has bless this land to become a very powerful country, that the United States is called on by other countries for help and aide from time to time and that call godly fear and love[reverence] and therefore God is very concern who is in the seat as President of America.

AMERICA—We as American has helped other countries with necessities when they stood in need and us as American step up to the plate and bless them with thing that these other countries stood in the need of and in return God bless this country America to become a powerful country who reaches out protect other in their adverse times.

AMERICA- The presidents of America after making a speech to the nation end there speaking by saying GOD BLESS AMERICA you see, here is a country that is recognizing GOD— am I lying or not but in the years of 1973 thru 2016, GOD BLESS AMERICA is being spoken by our president at the end of their speech –and when that phrase is used by a King or President who stands in power God smile- HE is asking God to bless America the country and its people —to me, that is a respect to our creator that without him[GOD]-we can do nothing—America—. Still small voice—If we as American can just stop for a moment and just listen to the still small voice of GOD and lean not unto our own understanding—so what I am saying is— just slow down and take time out and just have a little talk with God about stuff from time to time—yes, I said stuff-God will surprise you, what are your thoughts on this year presidential election do you understand who you need to vote for regardless of their circumstances— what would God say? Are you confuse, and you just don't know where God stands in this year election for president of 2016?

The still small voice of God is always right and just understanding this for a fact when he speaks in a still small voice if will be according to his word written in the Holy Bible.

1KINGS 19:11-13–this is God speaking to Elijah-when he was confused about something]—And he said go forth and stand upon the mount before the Lord. And behold, the Lord passed by, and a great and strong wind rents the mountain, and brake in pieces the rocks before the Lord; but the Lord was not in the wind: and after the wind an earthquake; but the Lord was not in the earthquake:- And after the earthquake, a fire: and after the fire[a still small voice. And it was so, when Elijah heard it, [the still small voice of God]—that he wrapped his face in his mantle and went out and stood in the entering in of the cave. And behold, there came a voice unto him, and said, what does thou here, Elijah.

And when you have a chance read this chapter of the 1Kings 19—You might be one who is just like Elijah who was confused about a situation in his time-but God spoke to him in that still small voice, there might be a lot of noise going on around you of this year election between Mr. Trump and Mrs. Clinton and you might not know what the bible said about this situation just listen to your conscience it something that everyone has from God to guide them in there uncertain thoughts in this life.

This is why the women are being warned by God minister not to try to rule over the men as kings and presidents in this novel that is being written also by a novice in writing but not a novice in knowing what the bible is saying about the women striving to rule over the man, my understanding is well advance in this area of the bible teaching God want the woman to be just and humble and beware of the pernicious ways.

2PETER-2:2-4 -And many shall follow their pernicious way; by the reason of the way of truth shall be evil spoken of—oh yes all because people do not understand the word of God they will then began to dispute the teaching that is in the bible about the women ruling over the man and there place in the world put in force by God himself.

Do you know that God does not want the women in the pulpits of his church, that apostle Paul made this statement let your women keep silence in the [WHAT!]-for it is not permitted unto them to speak, —-but they are commanded to be under obedience— as also saith the law.

Did you know from the beginning of time with Adam and Eve- that Adam's wife, Eve, had a problem being obedience and subject to God's commandment and I see even in the year of 2016 that some women have the same problem that there mother Eve had and that being obedience to God's Word—if God has said to the women by the mouth of his prophets to stay out of the pulpits and we see this disobedience carryout by some of our women in the holy places what about the other places that God is concern about such as the office of the White House where the president of America live and reside.

This office should always depend on God and God has intended it to be that way for a reason —God knows everything from the rising of the sun to the going down of the same.

PSALMS 113: 3-4—From the rising of the sun unto the going down of the same the Lord's name is to be praised. The Lord is high above all nation-[AMERICA]—and his glory above the heavens.

If the women and men can't be obedience in the small things of God what about the important things of God. This just one of the many things that I am pointing out- that I am striving and hoping that the readers will understand why I am writing with such seriousness I just want the world to understand and know that God is very serious when he said do not. It appears to me that some people are just going to ignore what God said not to do and do it anyway.

Like voting for a woman to be president of the most powerful country in the world. Do not people know that the earth is the Lords and the fulness thereof— [everything belongeth to God]. Do we not understand that the United States belong to GOD this is his world that was created and call it earth and it is all his that includes me and you?

Psalms 100:3 —Know ye that the Lord he is God: it is he that has made us, and not we ourselves, we are his people, and the sheep of his pasture—you see here another confirming of God word in which I stand on as truth. —I can only speak and write about what I as a minister understand and know of God word. So, I am writing about this 2016 Presidential election to let all people know that God is in a disagreement with Mrs. Clinton because she is a woman who is chosen by the democratic party to represent all of the democratic people, and even some Republicans as well who disagree with there on party member by switching sides because of the man Mr. Trump a Republican- that made this vow I will make America great again.

And I know that she will be defeated by Mr. Trump and lose this race for the White House as president because of what the word of God has stated from the beginning with Adam and Eve – God word has said your desire shall be unto your husband and he shall rule over you and because of Mrs. Clinton has a husband I will stand on this statement and I am not standing on thin ice either God word will be protected by God and He has chosen just little o me to let the world know the HE will step in and protect his word.

CHAPTER 9

Consequences

Being in disobedience has its consequences whosoever you are a man or a women boy or girl, even if Mrs. Clinton don't know the commandments of God and she will humble herself and pray unto God and ask him for this position she still will be refuse by God for this position because God cannot go against His Word.

In the book of Malachi 3:6–For I am the Lord, I change not; therefore, ye sons of Jacob are not consumed.

And once again the word of God has spoken which I stand on. SO as the election is closing in I know that the word of God will be standing strong and standing tall until the end of the world.

As I continue to watch the debates of the 2016 presidential election the polls are showing Mrs. Clinton is ahead in the polls on 9—16—2016. And this only continue to show me one thing and that just how many people in this country who don't understand God word and what it says about the female ruling in a country with such great power like the United States of America has God forbid.

And there are so many preacher that I am a witness to that do not understand this situation about the woman running for President of a powerful country such as the United States of America, they the preacher have a saying chose the lesser of the evil- I have another saying that is concrete chose the word of God say no to the woman that want to rule over the man point blank that what the bible says.

I hope that the Preacher isn't preaching from there pulpit to vote for Mrs. Clinton if you have preached such a sermon from your pulpit then I must plead God case and cry loud you are in the wrong preacher just be humble when you have learned of this truth and repent because of what the word of God has said about the women ruling over the man, God word is truth and to be obeyed by all men and women boys and girls.

[God doesn't need great numbers]-Let me inform you that God doesn't need great numbers to win, let just read what example that God use in the days of Gideon in the bible-[Judges 7:7–And the Lord God said unto Gideon, by the three hundred men that lapped will I save you[you don't need the 22000]just the 300 hundred]-I will save you, and delivered the Midinettes into thine hands with just three hundred men let the other [21, 700] people go every man unto his place[you see it said man and not the women who are out fighting like men like we have today]— When a woman become a KING or President of a certain country then she becomes the Commanding Chief of that country military-do we get the picture or can we see the error that the Democratic are making—America is a powerful country no doubt and I must repeat this again God will not allow a woman to have that much power over the man because of what the mother of us all Eve did in the Garden of Eden.

The Bible is full of events that has been proven to me that God knows how to win a battle with small numbers God sometimes does this to build up one faith in him just as he did with Gideon by saying go take your 300 hundred men and these men fought against the army of many and they won the battle against the Midianites. It all about obeying God's command and that's where your victory is. And the same goes for this 2016 presidential election God doesn't need the great numbers that the polls are telling. I hear Preacher and Minister teacher and the people of the public makes this statement that God is in control of this election and at the same time, the same people are saying vote for Hillary and the polls are telling us that she will win.

The First Shall Be Last
And The Last Shall Be

First—When things are looking bad for an opponent people has an attendances to count the one in the rear as done or finish and that that exactly what some of the big time reporter or analyst are saying that Mr. Trump is going to lose this Presidential race because of what the poll is saying well GOD has another saying in the book of Matthew 20:16- So the last shall be first, and the first shall be last: for many are called but few are chosen. [but this is a spiritual phase or saying]

I have been at sports events where one team is ahead, [the polls]- and a crowd is shouting for joy[just as the democratic voter are doing at this very moment because of the polls rating-they are rejoicing]— cont. and the other team is in the rear [MR. TRUMP]- and the losing team seemeth <continue to look bad>- to be done in and there no chance of winning-but out of nowhere they come back and won the game. Just as Mr. Trump will come back and be counted the winner of this race for the White House as the 2016 president of this powerful country call America. Because God works his best when the odds are against the one in whom God has chosen just to prove to the world who is really in control of this world.

THE BIG QUESTION

The big question remains, can Mrs. Clinton and the Democratic party compete against God's Word and win this 2016 Election?

Genesis 3:16–And thy desire shall be unto thy husband, and he shall [rule] over thee. ** take notice of this please. Who did Mrs. Clinton chose for her vice president to be? None other than another man, not a woman but a man whom she would be the boss of and rule over him do you get the picture—a man—not a woman.

O man, Satan is a bold one because he uses people to work against God in the thing which displeases God. — You see this is how Satan works he will find a people or a person who don't fully understand Gods word and what it said about the woman ruling over the man because they haven't been taught what the bible says about a situation like this election of a woman president ruling in the most powerful country in the world at this moment.

I think Mrs. Clinton is being used by the adversary and she might not even be aware of his tactic and so that he—[the devil]-want her to fight against God and his word- not knowing or understand what the scripture said about the woman ruling over the man in the most powerful position in this world she just might be a novice in the bible writing about the woman place.

When a person does not fully understand God and what his word says in the book of life— people will then lean unto their own understanding and do things their own way and not God- the bible is a book for your spiritual guidance and which is none other than the holy bible where I get all of my understanding and information of God so that I can write with an understanding of this presidential race between a man and a woman Mr. Trump and Mrs. Clinton and why God will be refusing her to become the next president of America of the year of 2016.

As a Minister of God I must continue to write about this election between these two candidates according to God word of what I see and hear of until it all over on 11-8-2016 and I know that MR Trump will be the winner and counted as the 45th president of the United States of AMERICA because I stand on the word of God which is nothing but the gospel truth and that truth teaches me that Mrs. Clinton will lose because God word is perpetual [forever].

And nobody can override God's Word like they do a computer or delete any of God word because it settle up in heaven where no one is able to get up there and erase something out of the book of life that they don't agree with, this world will pass away before Gods word will, you want to know why God is everlasting and he is that word that I been standing up for since 8-3-2016.

Matthew 24:35 -Heaven and earth shall pass away, [do we get that- this old world is going to pass away people-] cont. -, but my words [God has said]-shall not pass away. just another confirmation of God word being written down for our learning that will stand forever.

God cannot Lie-**God will never be found a liar—read this in the book of the Hebrews 6:18–that by two immutable—[unable to change]—things, in which it was impossible for God to lie, we might have strong consolation-[I can or you can be comforted]—who have fled for refuge to lay hold upon the hope—set before the us-The book of the Number 23:19.

God is not a man, that he should lie; neither the son of man, that he should repent: hath he saith [God], and shall not do it? Or hath he not spoken, and shall he not make it good?-Now that is God holy word and nobody can change it and nobody is able to change God mind on this election so Democrat voters you can stop praying for victory for the one in whom God is against in this year president election GOD will not hear your cry.

Ecclesiastes 3:14 -I know that, whatsoever God doeth, it shall be forever; nothing can be put to it, nor anything was taken from it: and God doeth it, that men should fear before him[is anyone convince yet?]-where is the fear and reverence-This is why God has inspired me to write about this year of 2016 presidential election that men and women boy and girl might know that God is the ruler of this world that call earth so you might not be found fighting against God and let me say amen.

Problems—With just 48 days left until the election day on November 8th2016, we have two candidates running for president of the U.S. a Republican and Democrat. They both seem to have some personal problem within, but I won't comment on them, because the newscaster is already having a field day but regardless of their problems that both candidates have Mr. Trump the man will win this election for president over his opponent Mrs. Clinton the woman because of the law that was written down years before Mrs. Clinton was born and this law that was put in place by God and is still very much in force today[ALIVE] and AMEN.

Novice vs. Experience

Mrs. Hillary Clinton is a government major she works for the United States of America government. She is a politician and she has been one for some years now—from the year of 1993, she was the first lady of our country—-thru 2001-thru-2009[senator]-2009-thru-2013 67th united states secretary of state. there was a talk at one time that she was a woman that no one could stop. Now I consider that she is well experienced in the political arena. Well, that would put Mrs. Clinton way over Mr. Trump ahead a lot by having these many years of experiences in the political world.

Mr. Trump-a business major but a novice in the political arena so that give Mrs. Clinton a 30-year edge toward the presidential race she has a head start in this race therefore the polls look good for now experience vs. the novice Mr. trump. Since Mr. Trump know nothing about the political world I must say he has to be taught some stuff yes, I said stuff— a lot of stuff about being a president and all those policies that he is a novice to [a beginner]to the area or job.

All I have to say on this matter God has got some miraculous plan in store for America to prove to the American people and the rest of the world that is watching this year election very attentive to see what will happen between these two candidates.

But God will be in Mr. Trump's corner just keep watching the handy work of God unfold into a victory— for the one that so far behind in this presidential race is what the polls are telling that even myself will count him as done in by the Democrat choice for president only and only if I didn't know God, but I must confess, I know God and know that HE will cause this man, Mr. Trump to succeed to the white house as 45th president of the U.S. in this year of 2016.

I feel that Mrs. Clinton, will lose this presidential race and be very disappointed with her loss on November 8th, 2016.

Chapter 11

Breaking The Barrier

I know that Mrs. Clinton want to be that first woman to break the barrier or to break that glass ceiling that no other woman was able to break through and to be the first woman to make history in this country as a woman president in the most powerful country in the world and its military strength that the United States of America has.

O yes, that would be history if it could happen, but this will the Democratic voter desire cannot and will not happen here in America because of God Almighty who will be stepping in just to protect his word and his commandment just watch and see.

Woman have strong minds without question when a female wants something that she is told that she cannot have that just give the female a more of determination of mind to do what is said you cannot do because it has never been done before— wow I look at this determination in another way -I just wish that all people could have that kind of determination to be obedience to God's Word, like for example when God says the women shall not rule over her husband and they will say thank you Lord and say amen other words let it be so.

For one thing God do not want the female-[women]-by gender running for a position that will put her in total power over the man which is none other than the White House as President of the U.S. at this present time-it all about the power that this country has that concern, God and for a women to be in charge of it will BE against his will and I must continue to repeat this throughout this book because people it is all about the Word of God and the Power.

God is very serious about this year election of 2016 for president because a woman that has been chosen by the democratic party is getting too close to the office of the White House that could put her over every man and women in this country America as America first woman president.

When God see that his word is being put to the test by men and woman he must step in and protect his word, just as men and women would do about something that they owned and care about so much will no doubt protect what there just like God is going to do Protect—His—Word.

This is God's world and he does care to believe it or not— and God will be present on 11-8—2016 and Mr. Trump will win this election and I know I might sound like a broken record if you have ever heard one before— it just get stuck and play the same thing over and over again and I must say I am stuck on God word and I must write like a broken record and repeat this over and over again the woman shall not rule over her husband and God has said her desire shall be unto her husband and that the word of God that I am stuck on because it is truth-Genesis-chap-3-ver-16.

Let us read some more of God word that is written in the King James bible dated-1611.

This is for your learning still—1Timothy-2:12-14-[Authority]- But I suffer not a women to teach, [what]-nor to usurp[takes a position of power- or importance-illegally or by force]-it is illegal for a woman to take the role as a preacher in a church or a position as a president of any country which is none other than a position of power whether it in a church or a position of rulership as a President because God word said so.

The United States of America is a country of importance wouldn't you say? and would you also say God bless America too, you see this country carry a lot of clout with God. -Authority- [the power or right to give orders make decision and enforce obedience]do we understand this scripture women and men to enforce obedience]if the women can't be obedience to their husband as a wife which is stated in God's word which is of and importance to God-[obedience]—what make the men and women believe that God want that person in charge of a country that will put her over the man are we feeling this scripture [understanding]-but to be in silence-Well there is shore enough a lot of noise going on in some of the America churches about voting for Mrs. Clinton for president of the U. S. that is an disobedience going on within the churches by some, when the laws of God said the women are to keep silence in the churches[man this word is so true and I say thank you Lord]-because I know it a lot of noise going on in some of America church saying vote for Mrs. Clinton.

For Adam was the first form. Wow I just got to share this piece of wisdom with you]Adam was the first form by God from mother nature call earth** -Adam was not born of Eve** but Eve was created by God from one of Adam's ribs which mean she was created from the flesh of man by God**then that make her Eve number 2**, therefore, she is of Adam-this can be consider as a chain of command-God have the power—God has the authority of this organization that is called earth and God choose the man Adam first and created Adam from the dust of the earth created he him first—num. 1—do we get the picture—once again let me say Adam was created from the dust of the earth by God— and Eve was created from the flesh of Adam and then the woman called Eve was the second one that God created so when does second place become first place-never]—first place is the head—second place is the tail and the tail always follow the head **so how can that tail[woman]— get ahead of the head—[MAN]— in this presidential race of 2016 and win** when GOD has made a law because of Eve disobedience that she committed in the Garden of Eden and for that sin God curse Eve with a curse that drops her below Adam which is that** head- and HE shall rule over her and all the other women that should be born in this world do we get this **the man is the head**women** and God want you to follow the men and not rule over them as a president**this is from the Head call God the change of command.

For Adam was the first form and then Eve. ver. 14-And Adam was not deceived, but the women being deceived was in the transgression

[transgression-an act that goes against a law, or code of conduct; an offense]—Eve went against God's law and touch the forbidden tree of good and evil-which is call transgression and Eve Adam wife did transgress against God laws and the rules that He gave them she was the first one to disobey God so she was in the transgression and this displeased God greatly.

So, you see the woman was put below the man by God and that law is still effective today.

But that seed of disobedience that the serpent planted in Eve mind that day so deeply, it spread like a bad cold or a contagious disease to all of the other women in the world because I am a witness to this disobedience and you are a witness to it also when you see a women standing in the pulpit which gives her the leadership of the church congregation and standing in a place trying to become President of America I see that seed of disobedience still going on today also.

When God made a law that said the women shall not rule over her husband and I know that God will not allow this disobedience to come to pass and the female candidate for the democratic presidency will be denied.

Although she was chosen by men and women of the Democratic party to run for this office of President of the united states of America I must plea God case and say that God will be denying their request for a women president -it all about the Power— [broken record]. and let me say that God knoweth how to deliver the godly out of this temptation.

CHAPTER 12

Godly Deliver Out Of Temptation

Let me reiterate on this title a bit concerning this 2016 president election between Mr. Trump and Mrs. Clinton- who does it affect if Mrs. Clinton was allowed to win the 2016 president election and why will God step in like He is going to do and stand up for the godly people of this country call America and keeping a woman from becoming president of the U.S.

Number-1-A President has a voice and they have a way of changing things even in this civilized world we live in—A president could establish a law that state- [just an example]- that will stop a person from worshipping God freely because that day is coming our way America believe it or not.

A women president can change a law that all men must bow down to them or put in jail believe this or not it could happen just suppose that a women that a women president would make a law that when a man married a women he the husband has to obey the husband and take her last name because now they are the head and the men are the tail but these are just some example for you to think about and to consider.

Even in this present administration some laws have change that is against the godly and Christian people that live in America, Merry Christmas is being attacked they want people to say Happy Holiday and get rid of Christ out of the Christmas what make Christmas happy is that Christ was a gift to the world from God and that what made it a happy holiday A savior name Jesus Christ was born to save all men from their sins and will not be ashamed of that name Christ nor to say merry Christmas and I know that God who holds the breathe in everyone nostril has got my back on this statement. Amen.

Changing of time: Time is changing all over this world men shall be lovers of them own selves.

2Timothy 3:2–For men shall be lovers of their own selves, covetous, boasters, proud, blasphemers, disobedience to parents, unthankful, unholy-the word of truth has spoken once again and these things that were mention in this verse are going on right in the year of 2016. When you hurt the godly people by banding them who is your neighbor and they are U.

Senior citizen in this country by putting restriction on the godly people so that they can't preach certain sermons from there pulpits and even the Christian businesses that are being attacked and they will be sued for not performing certain task that might be against their standard of living and these are the things that a President has to take in consideration and not being a lover of their own selves but being considered of your fellow man.

The godly people are the ones who are praying to God for safety and protection for all of our leader that is in this world because time is changing O-yes things are not like yesterday years when you could leave your house door unlock all night and leave your keys in your car— we got to pray more so now than ever because we need God and we just can't push God up in a corner and just use him as we do a spare tire.

The only time you use a spare tire is when you have a flat or the only time you pray is when adversity hit your front yard then the lover of them own selves want to kneel and pray to God for help—-pray before adversity hits our front yard.

If nobody else wants to pray then please I must say please don't hinder the righteous and the Christian people from praying we need our PRESIDENT'S of America to be God-fearing men o yes, I say, men, because God always chooses men in a strong and powerful country— that he watches so closely like America.

People consider this, we need our godly people around us at all time we need our church family at all time we need our prayer warrior at all time, we need a God-fearing president at all time.

This country was established on God-fearing people that called the pilgrim that came from a distant land across these seas to get to this great land that I call Canaan land-[bless land]- also known to the rest of the world as America the land of the free and the brave, then it was joined by other the states that were from around Virginia until it became the United States of America by those joining states that started with Delaware and I must say the United States became a blessed country because of its unity-united we will stand divided we will far apart piece by piece.

Divided heed—in the book of Mark 3: 24-25–And if a kingdom is divided against itself, that kingdom cannot stand. And if a house is divided against itself, that house cannot stand.

That's why it so important to spend some time with God and learn of him by reading and studying his word-[the Bible]- so you won't find yourselves in a division among yourselves like is going on right today in this year concerning our Presidential elections, because I believe a lot of people just don't understand the principle of God and the reason why Mrs. Clinton will be losing this presidential race.

That why God has inspired me to write about this year election of 2016 for president between MR Trump and Mrs. Clinton, because some things need to be clear up here about the two candidate that is chosen to run for that office as President, Mr. Trump is God chosen one to win this race for the White House as the 45th President because he is a man.

And I say this because of what the Bible teaches, Mrs. Clinton was chosen by men and women of the democratic party and not by God-who has the most power? God- or men or the women?]- I got to say GOD Almighty has got the power over this world and this Presidential race.

And certainly, the men and women chosen for president will lose this race for President of the year of 2016 and these are the things that need to be clear up. God said NO! Do we get the point as my dad Mr. Mo Smith will often say?–it is written all through the biblical teaching about the women ruling over the man which God is against because of what his word says and the power that this country has.

Now, I will say at this moment while I am Gods writer, God is showing the world love and mercy no doubt by allowing me to write continuously just to let the world know about his thoughts on this year election for president of the United States of America between Mr. Trump and Mrs. Clinton.

It's not that Mrs. Clinton is not a strong candidate for president because I think that she is well qualified, and she does have the experience over her opponent Mr. Trump because of her political experience but God has already said no years ago before she was born in this world because God knew us all before we were born and that just the kind of power that God has that He knows everyone future.

God knew this day was coming that's why he has prepared the chosen ones for this day-the novice Mr. Trump runner for president MR. MARK C SMITH -THE WRITER that GOD will be using to document and give the spiritual meaning of this presidential race, also he has chosen me before the I was born to let the world know why the democratic party will be losing this Presidential race of the year of 2016.

Prophecy: I know that the bible is full of prophecies that must come to pass because I have read of some of them and one of them are children shall revolt against their parents and brother against brother-Mark 13: 12–Now the brother shall betray the brother to death. [read the papers]- and the father the son: and children shall rise up against their parents, [just watch the talk shows]-and shall cause them to be put to death-the children today will divorce their parents because they are in a disagreement with the parents so they go to the court system and have their parent up before a judge and guess what you are put to death as there parent is this statement true yes it is [prophecies] they will divorce you and you are now considered not to be their parents any more saith the law of man.

But I have not read any prophecy yet out of the bible that states of a woman being in total power of the most powerful country in the world as of now and its military as a commanding Chief now there are some very smart intelligent and good women in this country that have done some good thing for this country of all nationalities of people that reside here in America.

They, the women, have even excelled to the top of the world most corporates businesses as manager and CEO but I must say to all the women that live here in America that's good but I hate to be the one to burst your bubbles but you are limited women and there is one office that you aren't allowed to rule and that's the oval office as A president of this country America it is forbidden for women to be president there by God.

God has great respect for America as of now, but you got some people out there that trying to discredit America with God by trying to put a woman in the oval office as president of this country is the problem. which is against what God teaches us about the women place, Women I look at the white house as a hallowed place you may work there as an aide to the President but God will never allow you to rule there as The President of the United States of America Women it is forbidden for you to try to succeed there as a president.

Consider this office at the White House as the forbidden tree of Gods garden-the White House—do not – touch-unto all women that's the rule and law of God, it is the forbidden tree that's in another garden of God call the White House do not try to succeed there women as a president of this country it has been reserved for men only by God you women desire power be powerful in obeying God and your husband—being subject to him this is what the bible teaches us —if you don't have a husband and you are a single woman be powerful in obeying God word and make him smile at you and believe me that's a beautiful feeling when God smile upon you like he doing right now at this moment with Republican choice for president, Mr. Donald Trump and frowning upon the Democrats voter and their choice for president.

In the book of MICAH 6:8–has shewed thee; o man what is good[thank you Lord]-and what does the Lord require of thee, but to do justly, and to love mercy, and to walk humbly with thy God?— Humble—We as men and women must develop and humbleness of mind, that will bring God closer to us as his people that He has

53

created in His own image. Humble only mean taking low and be submissive unto him- [GOD]-when a woman trying to be president of the most powerful country in the world at the moment which is none other than the United States of America at this time then she the woman is not consider to be taking low and being of an humble mind as it is taught in the bible —but just the opposite and that is called because high minded. 1PETER 5:6 —Humble yourselves therefore under the mighty hand of God, that he might exalt you in due time- verse-8—Be sober, vigilant: because of your adversary the devil, as a roaring lion, walking about, seeking whom he may devour.

Climbing the mountain—The oval office—I look at the oval office as the top of that mountain that some woman wishes to climb up to -in the manner of speaking-not just anybody will be allowed on the top of this mountain -just like heaven that is spoken of in the Bible, not just anybody will be able to get up there where God is.

It takes being obedience and being of a humble mind to God word to get into heaven just like it takes being obedience to God word to get into the oval office as president of this country, in which the woman is ignoring that obedience of God word.

Now, it seems that the woman wants to be able to tell the world to shut up and look at me now I've have made this climb up to the door of that mountain chosen by the Democratic party to represent them as the president of the United States of America I am at the door of The White House at the top and I am almost there and I am knocking on that door saying vote for me — but this will never happen at this time that door at the top of this mountain known as the Oval Office will not be open to Mrs. Clinton because of God and his word and the Power.

You as the candidate might have all the gear and tools to make a successful climb to the top of this mountain called the White House and there might some people that are behind you who want you to make this climb but what does God has to say about this position ye woman trying to get to so bad.

You might have all the tools that are needed to make it to the top of this certain Mountain—backpack- helmet-boots-crampons-axe- goggles-and how to tie a prusik knot and all kinds of ropes to make this climb a successful one-you got your campaign manager your sponsors your tv commercial and etc. to make it to the white house which is considered to be at the top of that mountain that I am writing about as the ruler or president of America. well women that prove to me you got what it takes to get there as a nominee for president and prove to me that you are in disobedience to God word.

Though you may have the experience according to men and women of this country— you also got the experience to be disobedience to God word which was given to us for guidance how that we may be pleasing unto God our creator—well request denied because you fail to be obedience women.

May I encourage everyone that is trying to put a woman on top of this mountain that I am calling the White House as President of the United States of America, obey and you will be blessed by God disobey and you will be cursed by God like Eve was cursed by God and that curse is still upon you woman and men today.

CHAPTER 13

The Rules

To the woman, I don't want to sound bias or prejudice against the women, but I must plea God cast— Until this election is all over on November 8th, 2016 and Mr. Trump is pronounce the winner of this presidential race because I am compelling by God Almighty to do so.

God made these laws and rules for us to obey and follow them and I must continue to plead on God behalf because he has chosen me to write and document this election so that the world may have an understanding why the women have been trying to be president in America for a long time and always have fail—just as he told me told me that Mr. Trump will be the winner of the 2016 presidential race for the White House as the 45th president of the United States of America because of what his holy word said and teaches—God word is true. A God made the rules for us to follow and obey to the fullest do we know that men learn the rules and statues precepts from the beginning of time starting in the bible days the rules of do's and do not—now women something has happened back there at the beginning of time to prevent you from doing certain things in this life such as RULING in the most powerful country in the world as the president of it seem as though somebody fail to obey one of the rules or commandment put in place by our creator-and guess who? EVE- when Eve ignore the do not touch rule of that tree that was in the mist of the garden of Eden she disrespected God first—then her husband Adam and kill it for all women to have a chance to become president of the most powerful country in the world at the moment, you just watch God word come to pass on November 8th, 2016[Prophecy]-when this come to pass will anyone believe that God ruleth in the kingdom of men and America is one of his kingdoms.

Why didn't Eve obey that rule that said do not touch that tree in the midst of the garden what happen to mess it up for you women that want to rule as a president in this country? Something happen— well Eve had a pet serpent I believe and at that time the serpent had legs to walk on or a tail to cause it to stand upright and while Eve in the garden the adversary enter in that serpent he was the best in his character-[clever]—[subtil]— which could walk around like a four-footed beast so to speak at this time and the serpent begin to talk to Eve and entice her to touch and eat of that forbidden tree that was in the mist of the garden and she did put aside the do not touch rule and ate of the forbidden tree that was in the mist of the garden and this is the birth of sin in this world and it was first committed by Eve the woman and for this sin of disobedience you women will never be able to rule as a President in a country that has the most power on this earth as of right now United States of America.

Eve show more respect to that creature than her creator God-It was the creature she pay attention to and obey the creature voice instead of our creator God and may I say women and men that why God has put a penalty on you women that you will be stuck with throught out your life here in this world-I know that some of the women have reached the spot on some jobs where they are the bosses over the men and women if this is so I must encourage you women that are the bosses at some corporation stay within your boundary and be humble because you might have men that you are over— but you will never be the boss at the White House as president because it is considered to be somewhat of that forbidden tree with the same rule applying do not touch because of God word and the power that the oval office hold here in America.

Genesis 3:3-4 -But of the fruit of tree which is in the mist of the garden, God has said, Ye, shall not eat of it, neither shall ye touch it lest you die.-4-ver- And the serpent said unto the woman, Ye shall not surely die.

Everything that I am writing about it is the spiritual meaning why the women have never been able to make to the white house as a president starting from Genesis to Revelation -because everything has a beginning and a start so men and women boys and girl it all started from the beginning of Adam and with Eve and why Mrs. Clinton will lose this 2016 presidential race for the White House.

Neither-shall you—touch it-verse-5-cont. —For God doth know that in the day ye eat thereof, then your eyes shall be open, and ye shall be as gods[gods]—knowing- [knowing some stuff] about-good and evil.

Now Adam explains everything to Eve about the garden and what God had commanded us to do and not to do he also gave Eve a personal tour of the Garden of Eden and show her all that was within that garden what to eat and what not to eat what to touch and what not to touch.

But the big question that I have in my mind is how in the world did this beast of the field called the serpent persuaded Eve to disobey God the creator and her husband Adam. another question I ask myself, how long did it take the serpent to pull this act of disobedience off? Did it take days months years I do not know but he did persuade Eve to mess up with God and with her husband and eat of the forbidden tree? [the serpent-lucifer-or the Devil-she was tempted and she did eat and some things change forever for mankind.

Lucifer: Who is lucifer? Someone may ask and what does he have to do with this Presidential election of 2016 between Mr. Trump and Mrs. Clinton or where his place or where does he fit in this election? In the book of Isaiah-chap-14-verse-12[THE WAR THAT WAS IN HEAVEN]

How art thou have fallen from heaven, –O Lucifer, son of the morning! How art thou cut down to the ground- [let me pulse for a moment because God is revealing something else to me] Lucifer was cast out of heaven to the ground by Michael The Art angel and his Angels.

[Revelation 12:7—and there was war in heaven: Michael and his angels fought against that dragon; and the dragon fought and his angels, **verse-8—And prevailed not; neither was their place found any more in heaven **verse—9— And that great dragon was cast out, that old serpent, called the Devil, and Satan which deceiveth the whole world: he was cast out into the earth, and his angels were cast out with him. *** other words— taken from the high living that he had in heaven and was put below heavens to this earth —which is his curse, and this was the beginning of the first war that I know of to mankind.

Look at the serpent that beguile Eve which had legs at one time some scholar even said he had a tail in which he stood upon, also like the cattle of the field and able to stand upright— for the serpent deed that he did unto mankind he was cursed by God and his legs was taken and now he has to crawl on the ground and eat the dust thereof.

God took his legs from him and now he has to craw on the ground**[when you kneel down to the ground that is below your height]-and that was the Serpent curse forever for beguiling Eve to touch that forbidden tree—cont. -ver. 9— his height and fame that he had**the MORNING **STAR IS WHAT HE WAS CALLED**it was all taken from him other words his place that he had in heaven was above the earth and he was cast of heaven never to enter there again forever he lost his place just as Eve lost the place that she had with Adam before her deception from Satan]

verse-12—How art thou has fallen from heaven, O Lucifer, son of the morning![do you see what the word of God is saying about Lucifer he was considered as a Star of the MORNING-He was way up there— this angel was a star to behold or to look upon-]—cont. -how art thou cut down to the ground, which did weaken the nation! and yes this all have to do with the 2016 presidential election—God is making sure that everyone that reads this book will have a full plate of Spiritual food for your soul that you will have an understanding about somethings concerning the woman that will be refuse to become president of the united states of America. Amen.

Do you see what this scripture is saying-weaken the Nations That means the world? —Lucifer was a created son of God-but so mistakenly on his part Lucifer wanted to rule- [does this sound familiar]-EVE the woman wanted to rule— Mrs. Clinton also wants to be a ruler of this country. **-are we feeling or understanding what I am saying to rule— Lucifer wanted to set a kingdom up on the north side of heaven and rule there and try to be like the Highest God is what his statement was, and God cast him out of heaven unto the ground also known as earth.

Verse-13-For thou hast said in thine heart, I will ascend into heaven, I will exalt my throne above the stars of God: I will sit also upon the mount of the congregation, in the side of the north:

Verse-14—I will ascend above the heights of the clouds; I will be like the most High[that God]-this is the trait of Lucifer-he was not satisfied just being a created son of the Highest God [just like Eve—wasn't satisfy]-Lucifer wanted to ascend above everything else that was in heaven and be like God without asking God first and when God found out he put Lucifer out of Heaven and cast him to the ground [earth].

Now Satan /Lucifer plan fail he could not be a boss up in the north side of heaven and he could not succeed to the heights of heaven-[like what Mrs. Clinton trying to do]-you cannot go beyond what God word has said she has a husband named Bill Clinton he is the head of his wife the woman and that what the word of God has said and God will not change it -Now Lucifer is furious with God because of his dethroned. And because he knew of the plans of God for the earth then he turns on all of God's Creation— so that God will be displeased with his creation called mankind- [men and women]—like God was with Lucifer. and now lucifer heavenly name is taken from him.

Now he is called Satan and Satan has another plan for God's creation call mankind that lives on this earth—because his plan fails in heaven.

Now he wants to put that same spirit in Eve that HE had in heaven as Lucifer to rule over rising above to be the boss ruler or president of a powerful country or be like gods is what he told Eve that will put her above her husband Adam-how long this deception take I do not know but Eve went beyond the commandment of God and was deceive that should be a god and ate off of the forbidden tree [and yes this still have to do with the 2016 presidential election.

Ecclesiastes 12:13-14–Let us hear the conclusion of the whole matter: Fear God and keep his commandment: for this is the whole duty of man. For God shall bring every work into judgment, with every secret thing, whether it be good, or whether it be evil. Therefore, I am starting from the beginning of the Bible because everything has a beginning that you may understand the present and what to expect in the future and at the end—that the mercy of God might be shown.

This is a proven statement Satan play old tricks on new people he is cunning he will tell the flesh exactly want it what to hear and this is call temptation.

Getting wisdom first—When Eve took part of the forbidden tree of knowledge of good and evil [ref- Genesis-2-17-] SHE the woman got wisdom first [wisdom-the quality of having experience, knowledge, and good judgment; the quality of being wise].

and with that wisdom that she gains from the fruit of the forbidden tree Eve got smarts, therefore, she became wiser before her husband Adam.

And with that wisdom that Eve gain from the tree she begins to do the work of Satan-the question that I am asking myself is what cunning words or ways she uses on Adam her husband to get him to disobey God command of do not touch that tree.

Eve did not trust the words of God or her husband Adam but instead she trusted in the words of the serpent in whom Satan was using who is a liar and a deceiver and the father of lies-she was trick and fool by Satan who enters the serpent and the serpent spoke unto her mind and she was beguiled.

John 8:44–Ye are of your father the devil, and the lust of your father ye will do [when Eve disobey Satan became her father of disobedience]. -He was a murderer from the beginning[Eve was a murderer in another way she kills a lot of things on that day-women are now drop beneath the man and now the man shall rule over you etc. -etc. — so now MRS CLINTON will lose this president race]—

Cont. and abode not in the truth, [Eve didn't continue in obeying God]—because there is no truth in him. When he speaketh a lie, he speaketh of his own: for he is a liar and the father of it. and that what thus saith the Lord.

CHAPTER 14

The First Lie

The first lie that was introduced to the world was by the devil himself called Satan and this first lie was believed by a woman name Eve-words are spirits.

Psalms 26:1—Judge me, O Lord; for I have walk in my integrity: I have trusted also in the Lord; therefore, I shall not slide. So, we see Eve did not trust in the words of God or do not touch that tree, so she slides far away from God because of her disobedience and he drops her beneath her husband and he now shall have the rule over you and your desire shall be unto her husband Adam.

As I was watching the news reporter walking around the campus of Hofstra University on 9—26—2016 before the debate had started a news reporter was walking around asking the different ones that were standing around waiting on the debate to start who they were going to vote for some said Mr. Trump and Mrs. Clinton and some said nobody and he turn and ask this one young lady who she was going to voter for she was holding her pet dog at the moment and her reply to the reporter was I am going to vote for my dog.

To close-Wow Boom! That is too close to your pet in believing that your pet can be a president of a country—it probably was just a humorous jester but this remark that she made brought my attention back to EVE pet the serpent which spoke to her and told her that should be as a god, Eve was to close-to that serpent the beast of the field.

I want everybody to know that I can possibly reach that God ruleth in the kingdom of men and it is God that chooseth president even in our time of the year of 2016.

Daniel 4:32—And giveth it to whomsoever he chooseth—and it was king Nebuchadnezzar that made this statement because he woke up one day after his foolish thinking that He was the man and came to realize that God does ruleth in the kingdom of men after God had taken his judgment from him and cause him to eat grass like the beast of the fields.

And while he was in the field eating grass like an animal of the field because God has taken his mind from him and he had a spirit like the beast of the field.

This is just another example of God bringing one that was high minded low to the ground. Stay humble do not try to take a job in this country that will put God against you and bring to the ground like He did –Lucifer-the serpent-Eve and Nebuchadnezzar these four was brought down off their high horse and cast to the ground by God because they got beside themselves and disregarded God— other words they pay no attention and just ignore God.

It all started when God bless Nebuchadnezzar the king greatly, but he took all the glory for himself that was accomplished by God and claim it unto himself and said look what I have done.

Daniel 4:30—The king spoke, and said, is not this great Babylon, that have built for the house of the kingdom by the might of my power, and for the honor of my majesty?

Ver. -31-While the words were in the king's mouth, there fell a voice from heaven, saying, O king Nebuchadnezzar, to thee it is spoken; The kingdom is departed from thee and God took him down and he went to the field on his knees eating like and beast. —And when you have a chance please read that whole chapter of Daniel -4- so that you will get and clearer understanding and just maybe you will see for yourself the reason why Mrs. Clinton will be denied from becoming President.

CHAPTER 15

The Bible

The Bible is full of these truths from Genesis to Revelations of what men and women have done to cause God to be either pleased with them or to be displeased with them for their disobedience and at this moment God is very displeased with the Democratic party for their choice for President.

Many people do not know of these events that has to happen in the bible which will teach you and give you a guideline to follow when we are in question— and I know right at this moment someone is in question about whom to vote for because of the Democratic choice and because of the Republican choice—when in question turn to God he always has the answer and that answer will always agree with the word of God that is written down in the book of life[The Bible]. I understand that a woman shouldn't be president in the United States of America because the bible has given me understanding why and it all about God's Words.

God's Word is going to be protected by God and the power that the United States has as of right now will be protected, God made the rule that no woman is allowed up there in the White House as a president it is reserved for men at the moment—God's eyes are on America like he watches a sparrow-[birds] because of the present power that exists here.

-he Pilgrim: When the pilgrim left their homeland England in search of a place wherein they could practice religious freedom and worship God freely then God touch their mind to get on a ship and go across the bodies of water until they reach a land that God has chosen for them which would be later name America and this move that the Pilgrims made please God and God began to move in their favor— it a wonderful thing to have the hand of God in your corner like he will be in Mr. Trump favor for the 2016 president election.

I just can imagine how the pilgrim felt when this new land appear in there sight that they were searching for and God said to the shipmaster dock here and I am sure that when the pilgrims got off the ship they knelt in prayer to God Almighty for their safe sail across the many bodies of water to this land where they would be able to worship God freely.

This determination that the pilgrims had it please God and God began to be very attentive unto the pilgrim mission in this new land which was discovered by Christopher Columbus and this act of the pilgrim cause God to move in their favor for them and toward this new land called America by the English settlers.

The blessing of the Lord was upon the English settlers and the pilgrim because God has given them a safe journey to this land where they can worship God in freedom. O yes, many other came alone for their own personal reason that has nothing to do with this religious move but the pilgrim desirer— it please God that there was someone like the pilgrim who wanted to please him in true worship and God has open a door of blessing upon this new land call America a land known that you can come and worship God in truth and freedom and for this good deed that was done God began pouring out his cup of blessing toward this country that it became great in strength and in power-so we see that at America beginning they started out by putting God first in there endeavor of life, then you as an individual will have the same favor of God with you if you just put him first in your life.

When a country become great in strength and power like America has it concern God who is in charge of it and what man is running it and notice I did said what man sure the women have been trying to succeed to the white house as a commanding chief for a many of years now but they have not been successful because God will not allow it –[WHAT]-to come to pass because it is not in the will of God for a woman to be in that much power over the man in the United States of America because of what Eve the first mother of us all did in the garden of Eden.

Once again, I must mention it all about God's Words and the power that this country has that Mrs. Clinton the Democratic runner for president for the 2016 presidential election will be denied by God and notice I did say by God because there are a lot of men and women who want to make this history come to pass—– [FORBIDDEN]-O yes it is forbidden for any woman at this time to become president of America God will protect his perfect word that is on record in Heaven and which is also written in the Holy Bible.

I am trying to give as much information out of the bible that I can about this 2016 presidential election between Mr. Trump and Mrs. Clinton as God will allow me to write because of it's truth to convince that unlearn person who does not know God personally— and I will strive to use these scripture out the King James bible dated-1611 that God will be giving me so you as a people will not be unlearned why all of the women have failed before Mrs. Clinton to become the president of America and why she will also fail and be rejected by God to become president of this year election because of what his word has said about the woman ruling over the man.

The Perfect: God still cares about this country America and I don't care how mess up somethings are here in this country—God has a concern because of the perfect people who are living and are alive in this country-O yes I did said perfect-the holy-the saints-the godly people who are living godly every day in this country that are praying for God to deliver the godly out of this temptation that trying to come our way a woman president for America God forbid.

I know that a lot of people has a problem with that word perfect when it comes down to obeying Gods word, the first thing some people will say is that nobody is perfect you going to sin every day they will say and yes this also has a lot to do with 2016 Presidential election because people wants their candidate for president to be perfect am I right.

When people don't have a perfect understanding of God word they will then follow their own way which could be against God word— because this year presidential race for the White House is totally different from any president race that we have ever had here in America times because a woman is involved for the first time as democratic opponent of the Republican nominee for the White House as President and may I say that it is not because of who this woman is, but because it is a woman in general that God word speak against.

And people need to have a perfect understanding of God word and why God will protect what his word teaches us of the do's and the don't out of the bible-This country was bless by God because of its religious standard and he has smile own us American I want to keep God smiling and let me say Amen.

Confirmation for God word. Mathew 5: 38–Be ye therefore perfect, even as your Father which is in heaven is perfect—yes perfect-perfect only means stop doing something that you have learned that was the wrong way and do it the right way with practice—and practice does make perfect—this also goes with obeying what this chapter in Matthew 5:48 what Jesus was teaching his disciple to do. just stop doing your knowledgeable sins that God is against and practice to do the right things that you learn from the book of life-[the Bible]—that you might be pleasing unto God— he doesn't mine and this is what is called living godly.

This is what God gave unto Jesus to teach to the Disciple and they were to teach the people and we preacher and minister of this year of 2016 should be teaching the same thing so that people will have an understanding about something such as who to vote for in this year of 2016 election for president of the United States of America because a woman is involved for the very first time in our history.

I as a person know what candidate to vote for in this year election because of what I have learned out of the Bible teaching and that will be for Mr. Trump because God is for the man and God is against Mrs. Clinton because of what Eve did the first woman to be created by God -she touch the forbidden tree of knowledge of good and evil—Genesis-2-:17-and for that reason God has placed a perpetual curse on the female that their desire shall be unto there husband and he shall rule over thee and may I say Mrs. Clinton does have a husband am I right— and I say Amen.

Practice righteousness—there are people who live here in America who believe in living a life free above the sins that exist in this present world and they are called Saints not latter-day saints but saints of God who practice the Bible teaching and the word of God that the godly practice becomes part of them and make them holy by the grace that God furnish them to become saint of God.

I was taught about this saying to live a life free above sin since I was young until I caught the vision of that saying for myself of what that saying really means—it only means when you get sincere about God and you have made it up in your mind that you want to serve and live for God on a full time daily living of being holy then you will have this yearning for the word of God a hunger for God and then God will make his abode with you and reveal Himself to your mind and you begin to put in practice what you learn out of the Bible in your daily living and the Bible become part of you also and that is called none other than being holy or a saint.

And this is why I know God will delivered the godly out of temptation of a woman becoming a president of this year of 2016 because he will protect his Word and He will protect his people that are praying all over this world for deliverance from a woman becoming President over us and I can smile today because I am one of those Saint –not boasting—but being grateful to God who has called me out of a world of sinful living that I was committing at one time or the other and now I can smile because I know that God is smiling with me because I have ceased from the knowledgeable sins and have learned to do well and now living above those sins and that is called none other than living a life free and above the sins that exist in this present world and if I can do it so can someone else because of who God is –Holy.

CHAPTER 16

The Blinded

There are so many Christian minister out there who are blinded to the fact that God does not except a women president in America at this time and maybe they don't understand that God will not and cannot go against his word and these Christian ministers seem to be blinded to this fact that God does not except the women in the rulership of this powerful country it all about the power minister that the United States of America has, minister and people who may not understand why this book is being written. -THE POWER. Suffer not a Woman—read what the bible has to say about the woman.

1 Timothy 2:12–But I suffer not a woman to teach, nor to usurp—[to take a position of power or importance- [the united states is sure of and importance]———illegally, or by force—illegally-definition—In a way that is contrary to or forbidden law]—and God law forbids the women to have the authority over the men—and yes may I say this also have to do with this year of 2016 election God don't want any stone unturn he wants you to have a full plate of spiritual food.

Now you might ask yourself this question—why wasn't the woman allow to speak in the churches in the bible days and even in this present time this rule still applied in Gods churches but disobedience has set into the minds of mankind and they just don't seem to regard what God word has said in Timothy writing and teaching concerning the women place just as Eve the first woman who refuse to obey

God command –do not touch that tree it is forbidden just as today president position it is reserve for the strong- the men of this country and to the women I may say it is reserved for the men. .

Now we are in the year of 2016 thousands of year later we see that some of the women are still being found in disobedience to God words and what it teaches us about men and women boys and girl what God has said for us to do and what not to do and you will see on November 8th 2016 that MRS CLINTON will be rejected from becoming the 45th president of the United States of America because of their disobedience to God word and the word of God will be perform on this day because God is very much Alive and another man will be put in the White House by God himself because he just can't put his trust in the men and women of this country to do the right thing that is according to his holy word in which I stand on and believe.

The man was created first—When God created humans the man was created first and then the woman second—by the man then being created first that will make the man supreme— [-AUTHORITY or an office or something holding it-] Superior to all others.]—over the woman that just the order in which God did it and no one is able to undo what God has set up from the beginning of time and God will not let his word be untrue God will for man and women.

Men of this country is always to be President of the United States of America as long as this country hold its power over the other country— but if this ever changes Lord have mercy is all I have to say.

We as men and women of this country can't stop the women from running for the OVAL OFFICE as a president that just call freedom or E.R.A. that the women have in this country —ERA is men and women doing and not God but men and women you aren't able to stop God from intervening either in this 2016 presidential election between Mr. Trump and Mrs. Clinton and that's called POWER!***and keeping the women out of the White House is what my God will do because he can't trust those men and women who are in authority to do the godly thing such as obeying his word and what it says about the women ruling over the man concerning this special presidential race for the White House –what so special about this 2016 race for the white house?—for the first time in America history a woman has move up to the foot of that ladder that lead up to the White House as a President notice I did say at the foot of…. but she will never be able to climb no further than the foot of that stairway that leads up to that oval office door— as the one to be a president because God ways are not like our ways neither is his thoughts like our thoughts.

Isaiah 55:8-11 —For our learning—For my thoughts are not your thoughts, neither are your ways my ways, saith the Lord. For the heavens are higher than the earth, so are my ways higher than your ways, and my thoughts than your thoughts. For as the rain cometh down, and the snow from heaven, and returneth not thither, but watereth the earth, and maketh it bring forth and bud, that it may give seed to the sower, and bread to the eater: -so shall my word be that goeth forth out of my mouth: it shall not return unto me void, but it shall accomplish that which I please, and it shall prosper in the thing whereto I sent it.

Now, men and women of some, I know that your ways are to try and put a woman in the White House as President that your way, but God word has spoken and that why I am pleading God cast on this 2016 presidential race and your ways will be denied by God.

Psalm-24:1–The earth is the Lords— [THE UNITED STATES]-and the fulness thereof; the world and they that dwell therein [that you] ——you see the scripture speaks here so how can men and women rise above the Word of God and prevail. God will not turn his back on his word like people are doing as of right now-trying to overcome what Gods word has said not to do and put a woman as a ruler over the men and women in the White House as a president of America. And I as the writer stand and depend on God word day by day it is my spiritual food for the soul that keeps me from being disobedience to God word which keeps me from sin.

CHAPTER 17

Smart Women

There are a lot of smart and very intelligent women in this world that was created by God since the beginning of time who has done a lot of good things for this world and this country -there are some good women here in America that are doing some good things and just as there are some good women out there just know that there are some devious women out there also and likewise some men also that just mean that from mother Eve we inherit sin by their disobedience toward God and God has concluded all under the penalty of that sin that was committed on that day** sin-the beginning of the of sin and now that seed of sin and disobedience is in everyone that was born from the beginning of creation until now except for Jesus Christ he was born of the Holy Ghost the Spirit of God.

Even I, the writer, was born a sinner and did commit some of those sinful acts that God word teaches us not to do. Until one day I was call by God grace—[man o man God grace]— to come out of those sinful activity and learn to do well and be born again by the Spirit of God that now dwell in this mortal body of mine and practice the righteousness of God which are taught out of the HOLY BIBLE from the King James version-1611.

And this is where I the writer get my understanding and wisdom of God who has inspired me to write of this Presidential race of this year 2016 because God wants everyone to know that his word will not turn unto him void but it will prosper in the thing where he sent it.

And if God has said the woman desire shall be unto her husband trust me on this— truly Mrs. Clinton will never make it to the White House this year or the after years because God word will be standing true when we are all dead and gone because this wisdom that God has given me to write about this year presidential election between Mr. Trump and Mrs. Clinton. and that seat at the white house is reserved for the men and not the woman who is trying so hard to get there.

James 3: 17–But this wisdom that is from above is first pure then peaceable, gentle, and easy to be entreated, full of mercy without partiality, and without hypocrisy.

I can only write about what I understand and know of God word and what his Holy Spirit will be revealed unto me or the revelation he will be given unto me as the days grow closer to the election and his Holy Spirit is only given to them that have a mind to obey his word and him [GOD] and you just don't pick it [THE HOLY GHOST/SPIRIT]up at the entrance of the church door and drop off when you leave the sanctuary. — God give you his Spirit to stay with you and abide with you so that you can continue to be godly throughout the day.

Acts 5:32—And we are his witness of these things; and so is the Holy Ghost, whom God hath given to them that obey him.

And I am confidence that God will honor his word and Mrs. Clinton who is that woman shall not be ruling over the man in this year election as president and as one of Gods godly children who live in and reside here in America my stand and faith will be that I know that God knoweth how to deliver the godly out of temptation according to the scripture which written in the holy bible the book of life I make my stand on his word all day long. His word has too much truth that the binoculars of his word can allow me to see the distance of a victory for Mr. Trump on November 8th-2016— Man God word is powerful it can cause you to see in a distance like a pair of binoculars wow!

Did you know that 59 countries in the past half-century have had a women leader in office as a Head of State or a Prime Minister or a President of it? And I did say other countries but not in American isn't that something to take in consideration— so why is this— well these countries don't have the power that the United States of America has and this power that we have here in America is because God has blessed this country to become mighty and powerful nation because of the reverence we have for God from the beginning with the pilgrim and the other settlers that landed at Jamestown Virginia. as America is different from the others countries in many of ways and God has smile on America because of their deeds that they have done for the other small countries and the moral standard that we have as American— so people stop trying to put a women in the White House as a RULER or the PRESIDENT OF this great nation of ours because God will not let this happen here as it is in the 59 other countries because it all about the power of God word and the power that made this country great and it all come from the great I am God and I am writing about America.

I just hope that when Mr. Trump become the 45th President as president that he won't forget to honor God for his victory to the White House.

The Hand of God: Stand back and just watch the mighty hand of God at work—the women so far have been denied by God to reach the White House as President of America and I will base all my theory on the word of God and why the women have been rejected by God to attain such a gold as a president and will continue to repeat these scriptures throught out this book until this election has come to an end and the word of God is still standing tall.

Men and women ought to bow down to the God of heaven and say, Lord, I am sorry because I didn't know that the women shouldn't rule over a man because I wasn't taught these truths about your word concerning the woman place and God being God who is full of mercy will forgive you when you admit your faults to him and that just the Hand of God.

Genesis 3:16–thy desire shall be unto thy husband and he shall rule over them.

Not even the holiest woman that is living upon this earth at this time— if she was chosen to run for this office as president will be refuse by the hand of God—God said no—The whole world is watching this particular presidential race in this country America for president between Mr. Trump and Mrs. Clinton just to see if God will be honoring what his word has stated out of the Bible teaching concerning the woman ruling over the man—the good thing about God word it settles up in heaven where no one is able to get up there to erase some things out of the book of life that they disagree with or delete something like you do on a computer.

THE CRY: I don't care how much cry is made by the public or the U. S. citizen or by the Democratic party members and it voter about their choice for President that she is the best candidate for President for this country she just might be but God say no and this spoken throughout the Bible concerning the woman so stop crying and stop trying to be a President in this country.

You can't get past the judgment of God that was passed down from God because of the do not touch rule—that tree that is in the mist of the garden of knowledge of good and evil—and when Eve disobeys and ate of that tree a lot of things change in this world.

Number-1-Eve is now in big trouble with God.

Number-2-Eve loss her equals with her husband and God drop her beneath her husband and now her desire shall be unto her husband and he shall rule over you forever.

Number-3- I will greatly multiply your sorrow—and one of those sorrow we will see on 11-8—2016 that the woman will lose this Presidential race—SORROW!

Number-4—You shall have sorrow on baring children and this is perpetual-forever.

GOD KNOWS—God knew from the beginning of Eve disobedience that the women that should be born throughtout the years would try to rule as the dominant force over the man because of the type of temptation that the serpent tempted her with—you shall be as gods—He said-that putting Eve over her husband in a sense but this temptation is a spirit of the mind to rule over— and this sin that Eve committed displease God and he said you shall surely die.

You see people what Eve did in that Garden of Eden— kill it for all the women to be equal with the man in the masculine sense— and this is one of the reasons why Mrs. Clinton will be losing this presidential race of 2016 just watch God's Words be fulfilled on November 8th-2016—-that opportunity died for all the women on the day that God spoke and said what hast thou done and EVE word was the serpent beguile me[HMM] and I did eat and mess it up for all you ERA folks and this is one ERA that God will not allow to come to pass.

So— stop crying people—we want to make history in AMERICA 59 other countries have had women president why can't we well it about the power of GOD —the power of the WORD— and the obedience to the Word-it all boils down to is this Eve disobey and it mess up thing for the women to be supreme over the man in America because this country is very special to God. O yes, special to God why do you think America has hold it power over the other country for so long there are a lot of godly and good Christians folk who live here in America there are a lot of good people who don't even go to church that live here in America we have a lot of good people who reside in this country call the land of the free of all nationality people live here in America.

The Power that Women Posses: The women that were created from the flesh of Adam name EVE have learned to be very wise I have come to understand that when a woman wants something she will find a way to get it—when I study the event that happen to Eve the first mother when the serpent tempted her in the garden of Eden I have come to realize that when Eve ate of that tree of knowledge of good and evil-[knowledge can refer to a theoretical or practical understanding of a subject/skill/mastery [wisdom-the ability to think and act using knowledge, experience, understanding, common sense and insight, especially in a [MATURE]- or utilitarian manner-the best action.

And when I look at these definitions of these words I have drawn this conclusion— that Eve the first woman that was created by God and was deceived by the serpent to disobey God and to eat of the forbidden tree of knowledge of good and evil by eating of that tree— she mature-fully develop in wisdom and understanding— and now she have skills— and with that skill she attain from the forbidden tree she was able to entice Adam her husband in a way that he couldn't resist and Adam did eat, —I have heard on one occasion that if you have seen Eve men you would have eaten the seed and the core- which is the inedible part of the apple and every part of that fruit.

For this disobedience God curse the mother of all women that should be born that their husband shall rule over them forever, so I must say again that Mrs. Clinton will be losing this 2016 presidential race for the White House to be a ruler because the word of God teaches that the women shouldn't rule over their husband and this rule still goes for the year of 2016.

And I must repeat that God knoweth how to deliver the godly out of this temptation of a woman being a ruler over His Saints— men and women boys and girls and you will see this scripture come to pass on November 8th-2016 when Mr. Trump is the winner of the presidential race and let me say Amen.

Potential: This book that God has inspired me to write has a story that needs to be told to the world, because a lot of people that are living here just don't understand a lot of things about God and especially his concern about the United States of America in which he cares for just as he cares for the land that he gave unto the children of Israel that are flowing with milk and honey[very bless land]— and when God blesseth a land like that— His eyes are very attentive toward that land— just as America is a land also that flowing with milk and honey other words it is a blessed country and it is blessed because of God who careth.

Deuteronomy 11:12–A land which the Lord thy God careth for the eyes of the Lord thy God are always-[AlWAYS]— upon it, from the beginning of time even unto the end of time.

You see God care about the land that he has bless his people with and God also is concern about a people who reside in a country whom his eyes are on such as American —and what concern him most are who oversees it as a president that is seated in the Oval Office at the White House.

This book has great potential for the future for the people who live in America and the rest of the world— mostly to our government businessmen and women who are in authority and to the leader of this country affairs I want to let everybody know to— starting with the American public and its leaders who hold the high offices position as delegates-Senators-congress men and women-Governors and President.

America is God's country I just can't express this enough and he does care who is in rulership here may I say— and this is just one of his companies that He owns called earth—O yes, this world belong to God and He does draw close at time and step in when it is needed just to protect what is his and what his word has said out of the holy bible that all of the scripture might be fulfil that people will have understanding that God ruleth in the kingdom of men.

I want everyone to know that God is very concern who is overseeing it too— and who is in charge of running things in this country of his-[God owns it]—- such as a President of the United States of America and people let me inform everybody you just can't put anyone in the White House as a president in God country either because of the freedom we have as American—and expect God to keep quiet and that goes especially to the woman whom God has rejected from ruling totally over the man and being a president of America. —because America is at the top of all the other countries in military strength in this world as of now.

THE COVENANT: While I was on a bus trip that took me to the Nation Capitol and the business people that I brought up here stay at the J W Marriot HOTEL downtown Washington 14ST. NW-DC. — and as I was sitting looking out of the window just observing the busy street of Pennsylvania Ave-NW DC. my window was facing the Ronald Reagan building and while gazing at the sights that were walking up and down the streets of DC it began to shower of rain and when the rain had to stop it left a rainbow in the eastern sky- up near the nation Capitol—WOW I can just see the handy work of God even in the documentation of this book that I am writing about even while I am in the Nation capitol Washington DC on the 2016 presidential election between Mr. Trump and Mrs.

Clinton how that God is touching my mind in a spiritual way. -THE RAINBOW- AND THE COVENANT.

On this day when I beheld that rainbow I notice that God is anointing my mind –[epiphany] concerning his promises about his covenant that he made with Noah and the rest of the world doing the 40 days rain upon the earth that is spoken in the bible and let me say that God is good about keeping those promises.

We see one of God promises being fulfilled even in our time every now in then when it has finish raining and when the sun come out and shine through the clouds and the mist of rain that is left in the air a rainbow will appear and that God let the world know that he has not forgotten his promise that he made with Noah and the rest of the world that he would never destroy the earth again by water and yes this also have to do with this year presidential election of 2016.

Genesis-9:12-17- And God said this is the token— [a thing serving as a visible or tangible representation of a fact]— cont. of a covenant that I will make between me and you and every living creature that is with you, for perpetual-[forever]-generations:

Verse-13-I do set my bow in the cloud, and it shall be for a token of a covenant between me and the earth.

Verse-14-And it shall come to pass, when I bring a cloud over the earth, that the bow shall be seen in the cloud:

Ver. -15-And I will remember my covenant, which is between me and you and every living creature of all flesh; and the waters shall no more become a flood to destroy all flesh.

Ver. -16-And the bow shall be in the cloud; and I will look upon it, that I may remember the everlasting the covenant between God and every living creature of all flesh that is upon the earth.

Ver. -17-And God said unto Noah, this is the token of the covenant, which I have established between me and all flesh that is upon the earth. And when God made this promise to Noah then he departed from the ARK. —THE COVENANT- this covenant is still in force today when we see the rainbow in the sky from time to time— so that letting me know also that the law that God made from the beginning of the first sin that was committed by Eve is also still active today so how can the Democrats put a women in the

White House as President when you can't get around Gods word and the covenant that God has put in force.

When God say when you see the bow-[Rainbow]— in the cloud that remind me God of my covenant that I made with Noah and every living creature that live upon the earth and me will say that every time God behold a woman it reminded him of the first woman that he created—and she reminds him of the curse that he had put on Eve for her touching the forbidden tree in the midst of the garden of Eden and that curse is perpetual-forever.

And I will repeat God will be delivering the godly out of this temptation that trying to come our way a woman that trying to be the first woman president of America. AND I will like to encourage all the godly people who might be in a burdensome state of mind because of this 2016-election for president—be comforted because God word never fail it is too powerful to fail it can't fail so don't worry Mrs. Clinton will not be making it to the white house as president because of the Power that God has and the power of his Holy Word and what his word said about our women who live in this world.

CHAPTER 18

The Eyes Of The Lord

The eyes of the Lord are in every place beholding the good and the evil. Maybe people don't know it is an evil thing to vote for a woman to be in total power of this country in the world as of right now and just maybe they the people don't know that God speaks against the woman in the bible being in control and ruling over the man with such power that the United States has.

Proverb-15:3-The eyes of the Lord are in every place; beholding the good and the evil—more evidence of God word that King Solomon spoke in his writing.

When the Word of God states something out of the bible that God is against and He has put a law in force because of something that has displease him, like the sin that Eve committed— the first woman that was created by God and eating off of the forbidden tree that was in the mist of the garden of Eden and this disobedience anger God that causes Him to put a law in force forever that goes like this— Genesis-3:16—And your desire—Women— shall be unto your husband and he shall rule over you[women]-the woman that was voted to run for president of the United States of America by the democratic party has an husband-so case close. —-she cannot rule in a country that God has anointed with such power that the United States has that's what the Bible teaches in several places throughtout the Holy Bible that the female is to be in obedience to their, own husband in everything.

Do anyone think that God will allow this disobedience to come to pass a woman president in America? Remember the Rainbow. God remembers the rainbow and remember God word is still as pure as the day that it was written down for our learning right up to the month of October 4th, 2016 Washington DC his word will stand forever.

What God wants me to do is to write about this presidential election between Mr. Trump and Mrs. Clinton of this year of 2016, that it might be establish in the world minds according to God's Word that God does not want any woman being in total charge of The Most Powerful country in the world at the moment which is none other than America and somebody beside me should understand this because women have been trying for a number of years now to obtain that position in the United States as the President of this country but they have always failed just as MRS CLINTON will fail on November 8, 2016, to become the 45th President of the U. S.

This also should arise a question in the world mind why the women haven't been able to become President of America.

ERA: On March 22 1972-is when the Senate pass the bill— The Equal Rights Amendment Bill— it was added to the United States constitution-which propose banning discrimination based on sex or gender this is saying that in America that the women who want to be equal with the men in jobs and higher position and with the same wages and benefits as the men are getting— we as women want the same thing and we want to be equal with the men in many other ways to.-THE WHITE HOUSE]

And God saw all of this before it came to pass when he took a glance at the future of Eve after the serpent beguile her—– and all the other women that should be born that they desire to be equal with the men and do the same thing as the men are doing and this is why God pass such a judgment on Eve, O yes, some women want to be equal and seem as though to me that many people in this world just don't want to be equal with God or his word and God saw this disobedience also and he put commandment in place for the human race man and female.

Can we not see the work of the adversary who opposes God called the devil? It's obvious that some women and men is going to go against what God has told the men and women not to do according to biblical scripture that just the way the fleshly mind works— and until men and women come to know God for themselves they will continue to disobey God and this is one of the reasons that God is showing the world mercy by letting the world know through this book that He has inspired me to write to let all people know whether you are a Republican or a Democrat supporter that He is in a disagreement with the Democratic Party choice for President of 2016.

God is saying no, and I will say no—no—no—you can't push this 1972 ERA amendment pass God word because it is too powerful O man does this word [POWERFUL!] sound familiar—anyone want power get God Spirit and you will have the power you need to obey Gods word and to understand his will that God does not except a woman ruling over the men and women boys and girls in this country as the Ruler of it as president.

THE APPARRELS: The women started long ago taking off their dresses and putting on men cloths such as— at first putting on men trousers or jeans is what women started off with dressing like a man and they consider to be a tom-boy—a girl who enjoys rough, noisy activities traditionally associated with boys- other words what I am saying the women have turned in the opposite direction from what God wants the female to be and they are opposing God.

And I will say when a women started dressing like a man she then will get the spirit that comes with those britches—men clothing—Masculine-def; —pertaining to or characteristic of a man or men—in which God is totally against the women who are acting or trying to take the place of the man— because God has created the women to be feminine—other words you as a women is fragile that's just the way God did it and do we need someone in the White House that is fragile?

The female sex or gender— and so we see today many women want to do the same things that the men do and for this deed women in pants who dresses up like men and the started acting like men-

[bosses] have you ever heard the saying I wear the PANTS around here—stating that I am the Masculine one or the strong one around here that just what that saying— means I am the boss, —say it not so—

Who started off wearing pants none other than the men— I will say that God is against the women who want to wear those pants of authority— and Mrs. Clinton will be losing this Presidential race-because being in total power of a powerful country is a masculine Job and America is a masculine country wouldn't you say— and God has reserved that masculine job as president of the most powerful country in the world.

Because God has blessed America to be that way -bless—with—power—O yes and God has reserved that masculine position for the men that live here in America whether you are a Republican man or a Democrat man— this position women is a man job and God will be backing me up on this statement on November 8, 2016, when Mr. Trump win this year election as the 45th president of America-yes!.

It as though the women are saying of today times to move aside men here we come!

We want the big house[The White House]—but my God has got a great disappointments for a lot of folks in this year election for president in whom a woman in a lot of folks minds is sure that she will be winning this presidential election but not in mind because I know that God will appear in a way that He does just to protect his word and what it said about the women ruling over the man.

My— my— O–my how sweet the victory will be for MR TRUMP who will be having the victory over his opponent Mrs. Clinton whether he knows it or not because in a lot of people minds Mrs. Clinton is sure to win but not in mind because I been taught through the word of God that the women are to be subject unto the man and this saying carry a lot of weight in God's eyes and it is true because God inspired holy men to write it down for our learning.

I also understand by the grace of God and his favor that he has given unto me and that is an understanding of his word that the women are to be subject unto the man and not the other way around— I believe what the bible said because it nothing but the gospel truth and I believe that Mr. Trump will win by a large margin so to speak. -[Prophecy].

In an event such as an election for President of a powerful country God has to step in once in a while when he realized that the judgment of men and women are poor concerning a country well being in whom he is concern about—that mean some people in this country feel like they can override what God word— which is perpetual— forever— has to say about the women ruling in that much power.

God will not be overruled by disobedience or the ignorance of men and women who are in powerful position in this country, I know I have made this statement before to the men and women who want to make history by putting a woman in the white house as president— the only history that is going to made this year on November 8, 2016, is that God word will continue to be historically true and God does not recognize the era of the women in this country and that is the history of God he always stands by his word.

God always want a different to be recognized between the man and the woman that he has made they were created differently for a reason—the man looks different a woman looks different sound different in her speech her voice is different in her apparel and in a lot of other ways is also different about the woman that God has created from the man.

CHAPTER 19

The Line

There is a line that the women here in America just can't cross and that line is the one that you have to cross over to make it to —The White House as President— because of the power that America has she the woman will be denied to cross over that line that leads to the door of the White House as the one that will rule this country as the Commanding Chief of our military and God says no and I say Amen. Page-45—KEEP YOU FROM FALLING—I don't want to image what this country would be like to have a woman as president with that much power at her finger tips O my my the thing that will be change and it will start with CHRISTIANITY because it is Christianity that speak out of God holy word called the bible against the woman being in that much power over the godly men and women who reside in this country so therefore I feel it will be attacked— but my God knoweth how to deliver the godly out of this temptation.

The law and rule that will be change against the godly people who live here not for the better I may say but for the worst that's why I been stating throughout this book God knoweth how to deliver the godly out of temptation because God knew this day was coming years ahead of time that this day of temptation will try to come America way and he has prepare MR TRUMP for this year presidential election of 2016 just as he has done in the past in the bible days when the children of Israel was in trouble God always have a Ram in the bush to save his people and the rest of the world and we as the godly people who are living in America ought to be thanking God and not trying to make somewhat of a history by trying to put Mrs. Clinton in office as president.

The pressure that we the godly and Christians people will be under if a woman was president here in America.-[remember THE Binoculars-God's Word].

The church laws and teaching as well as the godly standard that will be attack if a women was president in this country because the adversary of the godly will make sure that we are attacked we have already been attacked by this present administration by saying you can't say Merry Christmas they say it offensive to some but when trouble hit our country by surprise the one that denied God is the first to call on God Almighty and ask the nation to kneel and pray.

THE PULPIT—the pulpit is being attacked in a way—they are telling you what you can preach and what you can't preach they say it a hate crime and they call it a sin to preach such sermon from the pulpit about the certain sins that people are committing— the word of God should never be bound. —THE PULPIT-is to draw men and women out from there wrongdoing that God is against that is taught out of the bible which we preach and teach.[Pul-pit]is any in a pit today]—

I guess they are saying that I can't tell people this— it is wrong to tell people it is a sin unto God if you are voting for a woman president in America-it's all about the power people and the word of God which God has to protect and he will step in and do his part just as he has chosen me to do my little part as a novice writer who knows nothing about writing a book and informing people about his will concerning the woman striving to be in the total power over the man in this country America.

Keep you from falling. Jude-1:24-2–Now unto him that can keep you from falling and to present you faultless before the presence of his glory with exceeding joy. To the only wise God our Savior, be the glory and majesty, dominion and power both now and forever.

I like when this part of the verse which said both now and forever—right now God work is in motion to deliver the godly out of this temptation and keep us from falling under the leadership of a woman president.

The Math—The math of man states that Mrs. Clinton is sure to win this 2016 election as the first woman to be President of the United States of America they say—But the math of God word also said it is impossible for God to lie and this is why I have such a strong consolation in God word because God word was first the beginning long before man was ever born—before this world that we live in was create it was God word that created you and me.

THE MATH—If we do the math on God and his word you come up with the beginning of all things—in the beginning, was the word and the word was God.

St John 1:1-3–In the beginning was the Word, and the Word was with God, and the Word was God. The same was at the beginning with God. All things were made by him; and without him was not anything made that was made.

Now that's the math of God and the math of God will always outweigh the math of mankind, but this math of God tells me that Mrs. Clinton will not be elected for the 45th president of the United States of America according to what the word of God teaches out of the bible. THE MATH—

If America hold its face value with God men will always be a ruler here as a President and that just fact— according to what I have learned from the Bible through the holy scripture. But if God ever takes his blessing[hand] away from us American because men and women began to displease God by their ungodly deeds that they commit then we could lose our strength and power that we have as of now because God has turned his back on us and I don't want that to happen to us, do you?

But I still believe that we as American still are in good standing with God for the moment and he has not turned his back on us— I also believe that God will deliver the godly out of this temptation of a women being over as a president because of what his word said about the women ruling over the man and God is very serious about that and that why I as a Saint of God can stand on the word of God and I know that his word will not fail me or you if you if you are a believer of God and his only begotten Son Jesus Christ.

CHAPTER 20

The Book

Now I would like you to know in this book that God has inspired me to write— God wants me to let the world know in this vast universe that we live he does use the women occasionally that he has created to help his people and other once in a while. Look at Esther in whom God used at one time to help out the Jews at one time when a wicked man name He-man that was in authority wanted to get rid of some holy people or [church folks]— who honor worship God— and God anointed Esther with such a beautiful spirit and with that anointing that she obtain from God he use her too help deliver the Jews out of the hands of He-man–this guy just didn't like the Jewish people[or church folks]—that He-man told the King that there is a certain people scatter abroad and disperse among the people in all thy province of thy kingdom and their laws are [diverse]—very different from the way we serve and worship God—and like matter myself my way of serving God is very diverse from the other churches that are in my area and God recognizes that diverse way which is called holiness and righteous living according to his holy word.

I believe in living a perfect life for God—I also believe in living a life free above and separate from the sins that are in this world and so does many other people who obey God teaching and that diverse from the other churches.

I can only do this by God grace that he furnishes me from day to day to live holy—cont. Esther] ——neither do they keep the king's laws: therefore, it not for the king profit to suffer them-other word what He-man was saying we don't need those holy folks and Christians around here. -you see this is how the godly people are put in bondage by someone being close to the King who has an ought against Gods people.

These people can influence that king to change laws that are against the godly people and their way of life and teaching, and that why I say that God knows how to deliver the godly out of temptation of a women being President over us church folks that live in America— because the woman will change the laws that we have here in America. Look at the beginning of time with Adam and Eve how things have change for us because of what Eve did in the garden of Eden.

That seed of ruling over the men in this world is in some of the female race and it started with Eve even until this year of 2016 we can see that the women want to rule over the man, so I am saying that the laws will change if a woman was allowed in the White House as President and us as the godly people will suffer for it and if a woman was allowed to be President in this country all because of the power that this country holds which is a lot of power and a woman will lose her mind if she had that much control and power in her hands. but thanks be to God who is already looking into this future of the year of 2016 and saw what was trying to birth or come alive and he raise up a man of his choice that will defeat the Democratic choice for president in this 2016 presidential race and his name is Mr. Donald Trump and he will win this race for the White House and he will be our 45th President.

As I was saying earlier that God does use the women in this world to do certain things that according to his will and there are a lot of women that God has used in the bible days to do his will but I have chosen Esther to show you that God does use the women in certain area like she was chosen by God to help save the Jews from destruction of one wicked man thinking name He-man.

You see, I am not a women hater I just want the world to know and understand what the will of the Lord is and why God is against a woman ruling as president in the most powerful country in the world right now. —as a godly person and godly people we depend upon God for everything-health-strength—food—jobs—healing—wisdom— understanding—homes—clothing—deliverance-you name it even in the election of a President of the United States of America.

Esther 3:9–If it please the king, let it be written that they [JEWS]—may be destroy: and I will pay ten thousand talents-[term-several million dollars]-you see this— money is involved—of silver to the hands of those that have the charge of the business, to bring it into the king's treasuries. [bounty hunter]—and if you have a chance to read the whole book of Esther and you will understand what I am writing—it all about God will be done on the earth.

I am praying that God will give me an abundance of word to write according to the scripture that are written out of the holy bible to ensure the reader that God word is true because I know that I am a novice in writing a book and I know that I probably have repeated something over in this book— that the proof to the world that I am a novice that God has chosen in the writing of this book— a beginner just like Mr. Trump is as a politician a beginner when he enters his name in the ballot to run for President he then became a politician for the first time a novice.

But it was God that lead and inspire me to write this book I guess he doesn't care whether I am experiencing or not in writing but one thing for sure I am not a novice in serving and obeying God and his will. — now in that department, I have experience 38 years and I can say that I know something about God will. concerning a woman running for President of the most powerful country in the world and that is America.

And God is telling me to write about this 2016 presidential election and let as many people as you can know that He will be denying Mrs. Clinton endeavor to become President of America and all the other women who are thinking to do the same thing in the future because He has to protect His Word and what it teaches about the woman place.

And I will be using as many Scripture as I can possibly use to ensure the world that it is God that using me. And while I am watching the different debates and the different rallies I will write what I see and hear and judge what I see and hear according to the word of God and as he leads me until this Presidential race is won by MR Donald Trump.

CHAPTER 21

Derision

Why will people set themselves up to be mock and ridicule because that is what going to happen to the Democrat and its supports on November 8th 2016 when the ballot count come in and MR TRUMP is declaring the winner of the 2016 presidential election and many people will be in a derision just watch and see what I am saying come to pass I am standing on God word and its always true.

Psalms 2:4–He that sitteth in heaven shall laugh: The Lord shall have them in derision, all because people have forgotten to acknowledge God other words.

What God is saying out of this verse in Psalms, is— I will spell this out so that you can understand this verse-no. 1-Whatever God Word said obey it—no. 2—A woman wants you to choose her as the Democratic runner to be President of America—No. 3—This is considered to be a serious matter to take in consideration—No. -4— why—No. 5—God speaks against any woman ruling over the man with that kind of power that we have here in America—No. 6—you women have gone too far and God knows it—No. 7— and if you are that person who voting for Mrs. Clinton to be your choice for President— God said he will laugh at you because you didn't obey the Number one rule—and God will have all of you in a derision— other words you will be confuse because you thought she was sure to win.

This presidential race is the most serious one that I have ever witnessed in my lifetime and God will be proving it to the whole world that HIS WORD will stand true and have the victory on November 8th, 2016.

His Word and the second victory will be Mr. Donald John Trump who is in accord to The Word of God and will be victor over his opponent Mrs. Hillary Clinton who is not in accord to the Word of God and He will become America 45th President of The United States of America and I will say Amen.

God knows just what he is doing—You know as the presidential election day draw closer to November 8th, 2016 I don't need a meteorologist or a news reporter to tell me the forecast or the outcome of this election what it will be.

Because it is so easy for me to determine who will win this year presidential election between Mr. Trump and Mrs. Clinton because of the understanding that God has bless and given unto me of His Holy Word that is written out of the bible that I study from- The King James version Bible-dated-1611 where I got all my understanding of God and his will for mankind the do's and don'ts.

When you study God word— you won't be caught off guard and find yourself fighting against God like a lot of people are doing as of right now while I am writing this book[fresh]- do you not understand that God knows exactly what He's doing-sometime God will set in his Throne that is in Heaven and just be quiet and watch the children of men see just how far they will go against his Word just to manifest unto the world who they are that just don't understand Him or His Word starting with the preacher.

O yes, some preacher just don't understand God's word they will preach a sermon from their pulpits and tell you in so many words to vote for the woman who is the Democratic choice for president and not knowing or understanding that God's Word speaks against the woman ruling over the man but they The Preachers are teaching you as their congregations or you just a visitor who just happen stop by because of the noise that you heard from the streets coming from the pulpit saying voting is good when you vote for the right one she the best choice-Oops- no I didn't, yes I did.

They the preacher has just taught you how to disobey God in voting for a women president of America who God will stand up and denied her before the whole world from being in total power over the man as a president— because of what is written down on record for our learning and reading –preacher— out of the book of Genesis 3:16 -Unto the woman he said[God]I will greatly multiply thy sorrow and thy conception; in sorrow thou shalt bring forth children and thy desire shall be unto thy husband, and he shall rule over thee. Do we see preacher what the word of God is saying, and your husband women shall rule over thee and not the other way around she is ruling over you now that plan and simple to understand— the word of God has spoken so there is no way that Mrs. Clinton can win this 2016 election for the president.

Now Mrs. Clinton has a husband preacher-and people and all of the Democratic party and its supporters—now preach that from your pulpit preachers because that what the word of God teaches you to preach and if you are one of those preachers who has done this just ask God to forgive you because you did'nt understand these precepts of God.

That the living might know who are alive in this present world— God is going to prove to the whole world and that means everyone that exist here that He has the control of this presidential race— O yes, this presidential race It is different from any other that we that are living have ever witnessed and God will be stepping in to protect his word and what it said about the woman ruling in that much power.

And I hope that when this presidential race is won by Mr. Trump that the world will realize once and for all that God does rule in the kingdom of men and the United States of America is included as one of his Kingdom of men and this is one of the many reasons that Mrs. Clinton will be losing this year presidential race for the White House again.

If you don't study God's Word that is written in the Holy Bible you can be caught off guard and you will find yourself fighting against God and not even aware that you are replying against God like a lot of Democratic supporters is doing right at this present time— while

I am writing this book and they are making a lot of noise too vote for Hillary she the best choice.

I am not saying that Mrs. Clinton can't run this country she probably could with the experiences that she has as a 30 year politician but it is not her experience that God is concern with it is all about what his word that is written in the book of life—[The Bible]—has to say and God will stand up and protect that word of his so you may know as a people the truth about the living God that ruleth-[means to continue] in the kingdom of men and the miracle that is about to happen in this year election God is using a novice Mr. Trump to defeat the 30 year experience of being a politician and that will be the miracle of the year of 2016 to me.

He has said in his word in the book of Daniel 4:17 — That all the living may know who in charge of this world who in charge of setting up kings and presidents who in charge of taking them down to—, and to the [watcher] and that you and I and others around the world are watching but my God know what he doing, to show the world who side are they on. Are they on god side or is it man side? But I will stand with God and his Word. verse 17-this matter is by the decree of the watchers and the demand by the holy ones, [than me] to the intent that the living [that's you]—- may know that the most High ruleth in the kingdom of men, and you want to know something ?[THAT INCLUDE AMERICA]—-and giveth it to whomsoever he will, and setteth up over it the [BASEST]-a person that will aggravate-[VERY BEST IN HIS OPINION][GOD]—of men-it it's so plain its say men- not women and men, but men, men, men—— God know what he's doing, [if God be for you]—-

Now, you and I know that there a lot of people are against MR. TRUMP, GOD said the bastest, and in God's eyes Mr. Trump is the best man, that God has chosen, in these times that we are living in, whatever the job he has for Mr. Trump to do I do not know, but I will stand with God. **The popular is showing that Mr. Trump is behind the polls, but if God be for you who can be against you.

ROMANS 8:31 – What shall we then say to these things? IF GOD be for us who can be against us? GOD knows how to bring you to light other words [MANIFEST] just who you are that is fighting against His will. Amen. This includes everybody, there are preachers, deacon, piano player, school, teacher, theology. Oh yes, look at how many preachers and their congregation member, who are against the man that God has chosen to be the president of America, and then the people are for the woman Mrs. Clinton. No understanding, God knows how to draw people and reveal just who they are and who side. They are on too, but when God Almighty is for you, you can only have the victory and that who will have this victory with no doubt. The man—-Mr. Donald trump, and his vice president choice Mr. Mike Pence, they are God's choice and amen.

CHAPTER 22

The Beginning

While visiting Jamestown VA., these are the thoughts that have been running through my mind when Mr. Trump wins this election it will be the first time that a woman has made it into the position of becoming a president of the United States of America. Mrs. Clinton will lose and that will be history, and this will be a part of that beginning that will be made for the first time, and I hope that Mr. Trump doesn't forget God who has given him this victory over the woman his opponent and why.

For the first time, God must allow Mr. Trump to make this history for the first time also in America the [novice]no other man has ever had this opportunity as a presidential candidate or being a President to have a woman [beginning] for the first time to compete against him in any presidential election in America.

I hope that Mr. Trump when he has won this election for president will humble himself under the mighty hand of God and ask God for guidance because truly He's going to need it, that's why I am stating the word [beginning].

JAMESTOWN, VA was the beginning of the American journey. Starting with the first English settlers exploring a new land, that God has'nt allow the pilgrim to cross this large body of water to get here.

THE BEGINNING: Our country, America, has come a long way from where it has started from 1607 until 2016. You know, that's 409 years! America was first discovered by Christopher Columbus in the year of 1492. Do you know that this was God's plan to have a forerunner? For this country and Christopher Columbus was that man that never made it to Jamestown VA., only as far as the Caribbean.

John the Baptist was a forerunner for Christ Jesus. I see God plan being put in place for the 2016 election. God has always had a land like Canaan, in store for his people did you know that Canaan that is spoken of in the bible was a prosperous land just as America is.

America to me is a land that God has kept in store for his people and one day he touches someone mind to go a sail across the bodies of water. So, we see we are here in America to make history. Now, why I am in this town called Jamestown, Virginia the beginning of America? At JAMESTOWN, VA? God is going to allow everybody in the whole world knows who reads this book that God has inspired me to write— that this is the first time that a woman has made it this far to be chosen to run for president of the United States of America and it will be the first time [beginning] that God will deny the woman from becoming that president- who has made it this close to being elected as a president of this country America.

That the world may understand once and for all women. You will be denied from such power of that office to be the commanding chief of the world most powerful military and prosperous nation. So, this is the beginning, I hope that all the women may realize that God is on this country side as well some of the other countries and He is very particular who in charge of running it and God did say the bastest of men. [POWERFUL PEOPLE]

The most powerful people are out campaigning from the White House and they are out campaigning for the woman —this book that God has to inspire me to write is all about the woman striving for THE POWER over all the American people and all of the powerful machines is what I call them out working so hard trying to get people to vote for the woman that they the democratic party has chosen to be there king or president, O yes they are out there saying vote, vote, vote, well voting is good when its according to GODS will for that particular party of men, but this race God is against the Democratic Party and its voters for a reason, and I hope that all of the powerhouse and the powerful machine[people] will come to realize that when it is all over on November 8 2016. When God has chosen the man over the woman for a reason and God does not want a woman in power over the man and God knoweth how to deliver the godly out of temptation. There are a lot of Saints, Holy people and christain, who live here in this country and God cannot leave it up to man to protect them in this year presidential election between Mr. Trump and Mrs. Clinton, so He will step in.

CHAPTER 23

Men Just Don't Seem To Understand

Sometimes, it seem that men just don't understand God, because they are blinded by the gods of this world I call it worldly lust that will cause God to distance himself away from a person, and they will become blind to the spiritual things of God which give us that is godly direction in this life this is why the kings of the Bible always had a god-fearing priest or a prophet close by because the king knew that these Holy men talks, and made supplication and prayed to God daily and God has always directed these Holy men in giving the king's advice and direction in the time of war or when trouble arises.

But when men and woman commit those sins that God is displeased with it will drive a wedge between themselves and God by those sins that they commit and God will distance himself from you and your understanding will be darken and it is noticed even in today choices for the presidency, the choice that was made by the Democrats is proof that they do not understand God's Words concerning the woman being in that much power. History or no history, the only history will be made, is this that the woman that the Democratic chose as a running mate for the president will be denied because God do not want a female by gender.

Woman to be in that much power and some men and women just don't seem to understand.

Read this book and I pray that God will give you understanding that some grad mom or grad pa and preacher has failed to relate to you.

This message is to all of you about the truth of God, to the world I am writing that the woman has their place in this world, and America but not as president, that just too much power for a woman to have because He will intervene, in this election of 2016 because a woman is involve. God's Word will cause you to see through the storm, because it is very stormy out there in the political world right now, yes, a lot of folks are upset. WHERE IS THE LOVE?

ON OCTOBER 9, 2016, doing the presidential debates. I watch two candidates, battering it out saying all kind of stuff or things to make one another look bad, just to gain points with whoever —well I call it worldly ways no love lost between these two I see but I gather this is what they call politic I know that the media is going to eat this debate up in the morning like a hot breakfast or a tasty dessert.

MAKING WAY OUT OF NO WAY: I know that the media are already counting this race a landslide for Mrs. Clinton after last night debate. — well as I been following this presidential race since August 3, 2016. As the Lord has been leading me and inspiring me and revealing things to my mind I find myself standing in a maze of God will for me to document this year election.

God wants me to write and let the world know how much he is against this year election because this year election is a very challenging one to the American people because a woman is involved for the first in our history to make it as a presidential candidate to be a president of the United States of America. This country seems to want to, make a history, by a many of them that are voicing their opinion, why they want a female president when you don't understand scripture or God's Word even myself might feel the same way if I didn't have a knowledge of God word. But because I know that God is against one of the people that have been elected in this election and everyone else that want a female for president GOD FORBID! So out of no way God will make a way for Mr. Trump to make it to the white house as president even the man Mr. Trump himself will be somewhat amazing but the big question is this, in someone mind, they are saying how in the world is Mr. Trump going to win this.

Jeremiah 32: 27 – Behold I am the Lord, the God of all flesh: is there anything too hard for me?

God, the one that creates this world and everything that exists in it, because He is the Great I am—I say without a doubt that Mr. Trump will win, and a lot of people will be scratching their heads and say—Oh my, how in the world did he pull this off but I myself trust in God's Words that it will always prevail and be fulfilled in this present world because it is truth and God will not let the woman rule over the man as president of this country, America and that is of his Truth as I will continue to repeat this phase throughout this documentation about this election and as the world watches this election it will develop toward the man Mr. Trump's favor.

TO REALIZE: If everyone will just look around this world and just see this world beauty you only can say, to you that believe there is a God what a magnificent God that sits over us in Heaven and as each day goes by and God is always watching from above. As I travel from place to place around the U. S., I see and behold some of these beauties of God's creation.

When you see an ant, yes, an ant working so hard to prepare for the winter- without a leader, yes without no leader–that's GOD.

PROVERB 6:6-8 – Go to the ant, thou sluggard; consider her ways, and be wise: Which having no guide, overseer, or ruler, provideth her meat in the summer and gather her food in the harvest.

I believe somebody learns how to store food and victual by taking time just to observe the ant. Men or women are studying the ant and how they work so hard, so they can have during the winter months and shall we not think that the creator of this world –isn't concerned as to what's happening down here in America and around the world.

Also, concerning the estate of mankind oh my HE is so concern and when we get knowledge of Him you will then begin to pray for his will to be done on this earth concerning this election.

God is fully aware of what some of the American people are up to, and He knows the exact time when men began to be disobedience to his will too— oh yes, when we come to realization—to the fact that God is all powerful and his eyes are all over this world and what is going on He has already, started to set things in motion according to his will and His will, will be performing and this is what I have come to realize and to believe totally 100% that God will protect his word that it might continue to be true in the minds of people that has belief in his word and that's what I have come to realize, and that God will not allow Mrs. Clinton to become president of this country.

This is not something new concerning this matter, men think that they can do suit themselves down here on this earth and, just think God is going to sit by and do nothing. This is an action for God, and the world will begin to see that God is acting. We will begin to see His will be done in this year election especially with this year election because of the blindness of men and women eyes all because they do not understand.

WHAT HIS WORD HAS SAID ABOUT THE WOMAN IN POWER: I just hope when all that I have written has come to pass in which it will and is found to be all true that people will respect God's Words and what it said every wit.

PSALMS 128:1–Blessed is everyone that feareth the LORD; that walketh in his ways. Behold, that thus shall the man be blessed that feareth the Lord.

God is so powerful that when a baby is born god already knows that baby thoughts from the beginning of he or she birth unto his or her last day upon this earth.

PSALMS 139:1-3–O Lord, thou hast searched me, and me. thou knowest my downsitting and my uprising, thou my thought off.

Do you not know that God knew that Mrs. Clinton was going to make as a candidate for president of the United States of America before she was even born? Do you not understand that God knew that Mr. Trump would be the one that he would use to defeat Mrs. Clinton in this pursuit of the White House as president? God knows that Mr. Trump, a novice, in this political arena just to show the world in an open show how much power God Himself has, and that he can touch the minds of mankind in a way that even the minds of the people that He do touch even they will all be amaze! O yes, and open show and truly its already at its beginning a show that the whole world is drawn to watch just to see what the outcome will be.

I am striving so hard to compile all these thoughts that God is giving me to put them in a book form that men and women, boy and girls might understand the reading of this book; this book was written on a level that all ages might understand or comprehend from the White House to the person who sleeps on the street by some mishap that has befallen them, young and old all ages, and that's the way God wanted this book to be written.

God wants an example and America is that example that God will set for the whole world to know his feeling on a woman president and not just in America but in the whole world because they the people of this world are watching to just to see what the outcome of this election will be, but God's Words will he honor by bringing to pass what His Word has stated from the beginning starting with Adam and Eve.

For anybody to understand the things about this world and it's doing one has got to get to know God, just by picking up the Holy Bible and just taking time out and just to spend some time with God, by reading his Word. When you pick up the Holy Bible, and then find yourself a quiet area, and then begin to read the Bible, and your reading will turn in to studying His Words, and your studying will turn into a meditation and searching. Meditation will turn into learning about what God is showing you God will talk to your mind O yes- because God is a Spirit just as your mind is a spirit.

When you study his word, you allow God to talk to you when you read His Word it's God trying to have a conversation with you —and to you— and if you draw nigh unto God he will draw nigh unto you and show and reveal some things unto you, believe it or not.

James 4:8–Draw nigh to God, and he will draw nigh to you. cleanse your hands[minds]—, ye sinners; and purify your hearts, ye double minded.

God wants the men and woman to understand him— God wants his creation to be close to him as a mother hen pull her chicks under her wings to shelter and to protect them, and God wants us to be wise and to have the wisdom of his will concerning things such as this election of 2016.

Proverbs 4:7–Wisdom is the principal thing; therefore, get wisdom: and with all thy getting get understanding.

Because there a woman involved, and God wants everybody to understand his will for the man especially the unwise men and women.

Isaiah 32:9-10–THE VINTAGE – Rise up, ye woman that are at ease; hear my voice, ye careless daughters; give ear unto my speech. Many days and years shall ye be trouble[women]—, ye careless women: for the vintage shall fail [it will not come to pass]

This election of the year of 2016–to you that want to put a woman in the White House as president is considered to me as your vintage. Whoever you are that is striving to put a woman in the White House as president. The gathering together shall not come, oh yes, I have heard of and seen some of the rally in which the high-power women are speaking out. Oh yes, I know that the women want this powerful position as president of the United States of America, but God's Words says it will not come to pass.

The Vintage, this position you are striving for, it will not come to pass so God is informing you women that are so at ease and careless. Yes, the women think that they got this election in the bag as won so at ease to put a woman in the White House as president.

God teaches us from His Word the Holy Bible what we shall do. A blessing if we obey and a curse if ye disobey—a disappointment.

CHAPTER 24

Counting Your Chicken Before The Eggs Hatches

I hear that a lot of people are counting this race for the white house is already in the favor for Mrs. Clinton and she is going to win people are stating—O yes, the news people are rejoicing the public of many are rejoicing the big question is; Is God rejoicing? I must say no.

And NO—why set yourself up to be disappointed the eggs they are still in the nest just like an untimely birth, they hope? Hope is in God and I do know His Will, will come to pass. I hope that this wisdom of God's Words —will hatch in the people minds that God's Word is nothing but truth, and his Word doesn't fail—and it is certainly too powerful to fail.

October 12, 2016–With just 28 days left until the election day, it seems to me people are in a rejoicing state of mind that they are so confident that Mrs. Clinton will win this race that they are already planning their victory party. Oh yes, they are celebrating of the first women to become a president of the United States of America they say well all I am going to say is this, that some folks are going to be upset but when my God makes his appearance he will have them all in a derision.

Psalms 2:4–He that sitteth in the heavens shall laugh:

The Lord shall have them in a derision. It is sad when the Lord say that I am going to laugh at you for your ignorant and the things people do that displease me. Like trying to go against the will of the Lord by disobeying his will also in the way of voting for a woman president in the United States of America. God will show up and many will be in a derision. Then I will hope that the people will accept the result that will come to pass when God take his place and vote. O yes! God votes and choose because this election, God cannot and will not trust man or the women to do the right thing in putting the man, Mr. Trump IN office as president and Mike Pence as his vice president. So, I say that God will involve himself in this election and Mrs. Clinton will be denied and lose this event. God will vote by touching people minds. But knowing people they will protest like a spoilt child throwing a tantrum. Wait and see, all of this will come to pass,-[prophecy]- but my real concern is that this nation will realize that God does not want a woman in that much power, and not just Mrs. Clinton, but all the woman that lives in this country God will deny these woman that try to be a president in this country the United States of America. Knowing what I know in the year of 2020 another female probly will be running again to try to prove God's Word is not true—just read this book.

THE GOD OF ABRAHAM, ISAAC AND JACOB: This great God of these three men is the same God that I am writing about today, 10-12-2016 at 5:30 am [28 DAYS]. If you meet God in the morning he will be with you through the day and if take him on your day's journey ask him to go with you and you will find out that God is very much alive, and he does not sleep either or taking a break.

PSALM 154: 4–Behold, he that keepeth Israel shall neither slumber nor sleep.Psalm-78-65-The the Lord awaked as one out of sleep, like a mighty man that shouteth by the reason of wine.

These are the words document by the writer of the book of Psalms of David, and this King David realize that the God of all creation does not sleep or sleeping. King David has said. So, I must say the same thing doing this election, He will make himself known.

Yes, I am witnessing the polls, yes, it is looking good for Mrs. Clinton right now but the God of Abraham, Isaac, and Jacob and of our Lord Jesus Christ will appear. Just watch the polls change before the end of the election. God is an on time. God is never to late. He is all over this world: North, East, South, West. He has a lot of angels too, a host of them I heard and at the right time God will dispatch those angel out to the public of the American voter and just touch their minds because God's angels are minister spirits that do the bidding of God and they will help Mr. Trump, in the way that God will direct them and this will give him the victory on the 8th of November, 2016.

HEWBREWS 1:14–Are they, not all ministering spirit sent forth to minister for them who shall be heirs of salvation?

PSALMS 91:11 – For He shall give his angels charge over thee——[charge over]—to do what—whatever GOD desires is, and these angels of God can even touch your minds and you will find yourself doing GODS will in the way he desires]—that it will have you scratching your headcount. —to keep thee in all his ways.

I even hope that this book when it read by some man or woman or boy or girl, that it will also draw them closer to the Lord that they might realize that God is using somebody like me the writer, to tell the truth about stuff. Stuff that concern God in this present world such as this 2016 election, because of the woman, who is looking to gain power over the man——as president of this country the United States of America. There are a lot of Holy people living in this country and there are a lot of Christian men women and, boy, and girls who are praying for the will of God to come to pass and that His will be done in this election.

True holiness pleaseth God, unholiness or false holiness-displeaseth God. So, the few of us that are praying for the victory of Mr. Trump I know without a doubt that God will answer the few of us that are holy and is praying. People are so mixed up in this year choices for president that they are confused in whom to vote for and they are just so ambiguous. This word has so many different meanings that its confusing. Unclear or inexact because of choices. Confusing. Just like the word ambiguous. it is unclear what the word really means. That it's confusing because of its numerous meaning—even in the Republican Party and the Democratic Party. They both are switching from one side to the other, so confusing. Therefore, I say that God must come down and do what he does best. God will protect His word that for sure, and it's saying. I hate to burst a lot of folks bubbles I know that this election to some people is all about wanting to make history and that all it is to some people. History is something that has never had happen in this country. A woman president notice how there is an absent space I did that for a reason ——because it will not come to pass does that make sense well let move on—God will not change his mind on this matter by allowing a woman in that much power.

MALACHI 3:6 – For I am the Lord, I change not; therefore, you sons of Jacob are not consumed.

God's Words do not change. The words of Solomon also said in...

ECCLESIASTES 3:14–I know that whatsoever God doeth, it shall be forever: nothing can be put to it, nor anything was taken from it: and God doeth it, that men should fear before him.

Where is the fear? Where is the reverence?

PROVERBS 19: 20 – 21–Hear council, and receive instruction, that thou mayest be wise in thy latter end. There are many devices in a man's heart; nevertheless, the counsel of the Lord shall stand.

Men are scheming. O yes, out there striving to make one another look bad so that they can gain the victory over one another all kinds of devices is being used on both side [devices—is the stuff that you can put up on your opponent that will make each other look bad etc.

CHAPTER 25

Republican And Democrats Striving To Reach To Top Office Position To Be A King

If you just don't believe any of this wisdom that I am sharing about God's Holy Word, and you are so unclear about both candidates of this year of 2016 for president. Let me inform you, about some things…

I am just an old countryman who was born and raised on a dairy farm who had some very godly parent, who live what they taught us about being Holy, and taught us, 12 children, how to live godly, and to be righteous.

I have come to know God for myself and love the Lord God Almighty and believe in the only begotten of the Father Jesus Christ the Son of God.

He who came to save me and other from the sins of this world one day in whom I have come to know as a very personal savior to me and He has taught me some things about His Word.

So, I can truly say so humbly that I know some things about God's will concerning the estate of mankind and what displeased God and what does please him.

So, may I humbly say as God has inspired me, so I am writing for the first time in my life my very first book I am just a novice— by reading this book anybody can see that a beginner is writing all this. A novice in writing yes but not a novice in serving God for 38 years. I've been living for the Lord, and I do know that gives me somewhat of a credibility in the understanding of God's word, just to let the world know that God is against one person whom is the chosen person by the Democrats to run for president – a woman. To the people that are so unlearn about God's Will for this country that they are so foolishly thinking and trying to put a woman over the men in this country as president.

But my God knoweth how to deliver the godly out of this temptation because God sitteth on high and he looketh low and He knows at all time what man is up to so mister man and miss's woman you can't pull the wool over God's eyes because He knows just what you are up to.

MR. MAN–MISS FEMALE

ISAIAH 40: 21 – 23–Have ye not known? have ye not heard? hath it not been told you from the beginning? have you not understood from the foundation of the earth? It is he that sitteth upon the circle of the earth. Watching the earth revolve, and the inhabitants thereof are as grasshoppers; that stretches out the heavens as a curtain, and spreadeth them out as a tent to dwell in: That bringeth the princes to nothing: he maketh the judges of the earth as vanity.

Can we not understand what God is saying right here your judgment democratic voter is in vain? Yea, they shall not be planted your votes will not put Mrs. Clinton in office. You see, here it said they shall not be planted [DEMOCRATS]— your desire for a woman president [SHALL NOT]— be planted it will not come to pass] they shall not be sown.

I heard of these private meeting by a certain individual trying to see how they can get a woman in office as president of the United States of America. Are you trying to please the ERA movement? Are you trying to please the women of this country? Yea they shall not be sown [MAN O MAN THIS IS POWERFUL-GOD HAS SAID YE

WON'T BE SOWN OR TAKE ROOT]—[WOMAN]] their stock shall not take root in the earth:

God will be rejecting your desire to put a woman in the White House as a ruler— WHAT? —DID YOU GET THAT? and he shall also Blow upon them and they shall wither, and the whirlwind shall take them away as stubble. Do you mean that God can do this kind of stuff? Yes! God can do this and so much more He is able to do just that what His word has said.

Consider it done. So, let this be cook in your minds. Done. Well done.

All of this is in this year election. Make it so that their desire to make a woman president of this country not to take root.

God's Word just don't change. This Word was established at the beginning of Adam and Eve and God still means what He has said from the beginning until now, everybody got their proper place and that is for the woman to be subject unto the man and he shall rule over you, and that's what thus sayeth the Lord are you reading, And getting all this wisdom that God has given this old countryman to give unto you.

The subject, paragraph, the sentence, the phases and the title about this 2016 election for president. God knoweth how to deliver the godly out of temptation. The Lord have so much to say, and I have to write it down. Well I must continue writing.

ISAIAH 40: 29–He giveth power to the faint, and to them that have no might he increaseth strength.

You see, Mr. Trump might look faint, but God said He will increase his strenght in the polls just watch. God doesn't lie. God ruleth in the kingdom of men. God ruleth the heaven. He is above all.

I've had study this situation of a woman trying to be president of the most powerful country in this world and I have to agree with God word and what it has to say about Mrs. Clinton running for the presidency of this country and God has allowed me to write about what he wants the world to know about the woman that running for president in this country.

PROVERBS 21:1–The king's heart is in the hand of the Lord, as a river of water: he turneth it whithersoever he will.

Now if a king doesn't regard God, it has put the godly people in somewhat of jeopardy. the kings and presidents who are in power and has the rule over us as citizen of that country. Why? You see, some kings or ruler has an ought against the godly people whom live in this world and even in this country itself; America— I have heard of the injustice throughout the years that has been done unto them.

The gospel of Jesus Christ has been under attack even in this year of 2016—laws have been changed to afflict the preaching of the gospel that comes from our pulpits, and some Christian businesses as well have been attacked but we must obey God rather than man.

St. Peter and other apostle was commanded not to preach Christ in the region that they were in which was Jerusalem because they were healing some folks of their diseases and sickness but the high priest got mad with indignation-of somewhat, who wouldn't be glad for folk to be relieved of their sickness, well evidently the high priest which was a ruler at that time who had the power to put you in prison.

Acts 5: 17-18–Then the high priest rose up, and all they that was with which is the sect of the SAD-DU-CESS and were filled with indignation. And laid their hands on the apostle, and put them in the common prison, and command them not to preach in that name around here.

TODAY MERRY CHRISTMAS IS BEING ATTACKED BY WHO?

Yes! "Merry Christmas!" The 2016 administration of some do not want you to say "Merry Christmas" they say it is offensive to some]

Acts 5: 19–Then Peter and the other apostle answer and said, we ought to obey God rather than men.

And the same thing is still happening today religious folk is being put in jail for doing the righteous and godly thing that pleaseth God.

God knows if a woman was let in the White House, laws are going to change that would affect the godly people in this country, but God knew all of this from the beginning of time when he gave command unto Adam and his wife Eve do not touch the tree that in the mist of the sins.

GENESIS 2: 15-17–The Lord God took the man and put him in the Garden of Eden to work it and take care of it. 16 And the Lord God commanded the man, "You are free to eat from any tree in the garden; 17 but you must not eat from the tree of the knowledge of good and evil, for when you eat from it you will certainly die."

And when Eve was deceived by the devil that enter the serpent. To entice Eve to touch, to feel, and then to eat of the forbidden tree. Then when God was of aware what was done by Adam's wife Eve then God did something else and that was He took a look into the future of the world timeline and to all of the people that would be opposing his commandment, and saw where in that the woman was going to change in a way that will be against Him, all because of that seed of disobedience that the serpent place in Eve mind that she could be as gods someone might ask what is this God that the serpent tempted Eve with— someone who admires a lot or too much of something. Eve wanted more than what she already had.

The woman today has become gods to them own selves. When they go against what God has said in his Word not to do—and that disobedience is considered to be your god—whether it's a house job men women clothes and etc. If God speaks against it and you decided in your mind forget God I am my own person, well, you have just become a god by your disobedience—anything that you put above God word has become your god. That will cause the woman and men to change in so many ways that God himself would be displeased with their ways, and when God saw that the women desire will begin to change and look and dress up like men and men also will change and dress like woman and God also saw that the woman wanted to rule over the man and fight in the same battle as a soldier as a man and wanted to be kings and priest, minister, pastor and even run for kings and president.

God also saw the look into the future of a very smart business minded women that would arise in the in the 19th century who would run for president of the year 2016 election that was seeking for that power that was once offer to Eve the first woman that was created by God— and all the other women that should be born in the future. Because Eve was tempted in a way that was so, enticing that the adversary told her that she would be as gods. In that case if we look at that temptation that Satan offer and tempted Eve with closely, that will then put her Eve—The WOMEN— over and above the man which was only a temptation of the mind.

CHAPTER 26

Temptation Was Offered

What kind of temptation was offered some may say?

For a beginner it was a lie, the very first lie that was told on this Earth as known to mankind, and Eve believed the serpent's lie–the beast of the field–and the seed that he planted in her mind to be as gods— that was the lie. It was all a lie. Then God investigate the future of all the woman that should be born, and in that future what He saw displease Him, of what He saw concerning what the women wanted to do in the future, and their desires, and determination that they had in mind. God knew then that He had to make a law that will stand forever.

Then God past judgment on man and women and knew that woman has that seed [BRANDED] in her. She was bitten by the beast of the field and poison and this poison was introduced and absorb in the mind of Eve of ruling over the man, this poison that the serpent use was not liquid but a spirit of deception. A lie a bald face lie.

How many of you have ever been deceived or been lied to? That temptation of the devil to be as gods was a lie and that seed still is in the women today to preside. This is how sin enter this world, by the disobedience of the first woman that was created–Eve. So, God said; your desire shall be unto your husband and he shall rule over you.

I know that the woman is very smart; just as smarter as some of the men are but God said; there will be the great sorrow to the women –greatly—with all that smartness that the woman has, you never will be able to rule in this country the United States of America as a president.

God can do that— as he was observing the future of America before it was a known country to the English settlers that will be born in the future that will be pleasing to him and this country shall be a very prosperous country full of all kinds of resources and with power and a lot of power and that country was called first TUTTLE ISLAND at one time by the native Indians but later name America by Christopher Columbus.

The forerunner is what I called him- who never made it to JAMESTOWN, VA. SHORES. So, I say to the women; I don't care how hard you try to win, over God's command you will only lose and that's sorrow for the women that reside hereto be in authority as the President of the USA.

Therefore, the woman of this country needs to know that God does not want the woman in that much power. When I hear a woman telling a man you don't tell me what to do I see that spirit of Eve. To be dominant over the man. God's Words still remain in power today–as of October 16, 2016 6:30-am—as being a truth.

God's Words will be justified on that day of November 8, 2016, and I hope that the world may know and understand that God's Word is always going to prevail and stand true, and God can show no weakness in which he is not weak. I know that the women want to be liberal open to all their new option and especially political change, well it won't happen. The politician of a political party might vote for you to be, a running mate or candidate for that position as president but God said No!

To you becoming president of America, you cannot get away from God's Words and what it states and what it said and what it means, and I say AMEN!

Sure, the favor is for Mrs. Clinton— looks good for the Democratic party right now and to the world that is watching, but God knows how to show the world just how many people who just do not go to church or how many preachers out there that just do not know Him or understand the will of the Lord. I can say that God will deliver the godly out of this temptation because he knows just how to do it too. Nobody can compete against God and win. When GOD is for that individual you are going to have the victory and I will say that Mr. Trump and his smart choice for vice president, Mike Pence are the men that God is for and they will win the election as president for the Republican Party on November 8, 2016— it's all in The Bible— it is written in the volume of the book. O yes, it's all on record for our learning.

ISAIAH 34:16–Seek ye out the book of the Lord and read: no one of these shall fail.

The fact is that people are not reading God's Words, therefore there understanding of certain things are just not clear. God create everything for his purpose and HIS glory. O yes, to the women I may say that you have your place in this world God made you for a purpose I know you expect me to say in the kitchen and in the house-bearing children. Helping where ever is allowed by God for you to help— women have all kind of good jobs in this world where they are a good help to men and even doing things that God is pleased with just helping out where ever they can, but God has limited you to one thing that you cannot touch, and that's the most powerful spot in this world and in this country America, as God forbid!

THE WORLD IS CHANGING (PEOPLE): I know since the world was created, changes began to set in motion day by day, months and years people are populating all around the world, and some people are changing to whatever that suit them. Some even are forgetting to have just a little talk with God and when people forget to talk with God, then they will surely drift away from him and began to follow their own pernicious ways, not everybody but there are some who are changing.

When this individual wants changes, they then begin to want changes in the world or may I say a county in which we live in and that is America to suit themselves, so then they begin to look for the spot that holds, power wherein they can gain friendship with that person in power and then they move in to position so that they can influence people minds for that particular change and we are witness to these things in this world. Some of the changes are good but some are not good, and they will even adopt a law [THE RESTROOM LAW—WAS A CHANGE THAT I HAVE SEEN. —MAN / FEMALE/USING THE SAME BATHROOM-NO PRIVACY.]

They will compel you to do or be fine or jail, so we see laws have been changed because people are changing but one law that will never be changed and that's the law that God put upon the women. God saw what the women were going to do when he investigates the future of Eve and one thing that He did see was that women will begin to change their apparel and began to wear men garment, and likewise some of the men also was changing and putting on women garment and then God began to give commandment -laws -precepts and statues that will address these changes that mankind desire to do.

DEUTERONOMY 22:5 – The woman shall not wear that pertaineth unto a man, neither shall a man put on woman, as garment: for all that do so are abomination.

A THING THAT CAUSES DISGUSTING OR HATRED: If a woman is wearing that, which is pertaining to men, then she is in an abomination unto God. So, how can god let someone in the white house whom he is disgusted with and is an abomination to him? Something that is disgusting to him. Some blinded mind preacher out there will say that don't mean that. O yes, it means exactly what I have just written because God has got my back on this—unto the Lord thy God.

Now God shows Moses and gave him a vision of the future how that the woman and men will begin to change so He gave these commandments to Moses to prophecies on and preach and teach the children of Israel what they could do to please God, and what they couldn't do.

A lot of things has changed for the female in this world today, and therefore the women feel as though they have just as much right to be president in this country than anybody else—well I hate to burst the bubbles men and women you might have changed some laws and made a way for you to run for that position. O, but my God will protect his command concerning this matter, and it is a matter that he will a just himself personally, and that is the oval office as president of the United States of America.

It is for men only. This position will not become your god women and I want the world to know that there will be no nepotism.

It's all and all about the power ladies. O yes, the power and god will not let you attain or achieve. Its changes have taken place into today society no doubt, but I want all to realize that God's Words, will not change and it does not lie— it's nothing but the gospel truth.

OMNIPOTENT: Having unlimited power able to do anything all. Powerful Almighty Supreme Most High. The first and the last the beginning and the end. I have just described our God who is the creator of us all—and all that he asks of us that are created in His image his creation is to obey and to believe in him we are all God's children no doubt.

Hold your hand up to your mouth and blow into your hands— you see—that's the breath of God that he has given you and everybody else—that's the power of God that you have of him so therefore you are a part of God whether you like it or not you are God's property.

All God ask is for us to be obedient to His will and to walk humbly before Him. Well I guess somebody didn't get that message because this would seem to me to be out of control. O yes, how is it that man feel like he can go against God command and put a woman in the White House as president. God knows everything. He is omnipotent if anybody wants God to be on their side in this year election of the year of 2016, just stand with His word and His word only. Points to one person and that is Mr. Trump for the president and you will be victorious in your endeavor. The election day is ending, and all the world will witness this great event of the woman who is chosen to run for president by the democratic party whom will be denied—- by GOD THE OMNIPOTENT.

God cannot and will not allow her to win, because Eve took it all away from all the woman, I can't stress or say this enough. Yes your desire woman to rule over the man, and that is a spirit that they the woman inherit from Eve and Eve got that spirit from -Lucifer-Satan-the serpent the –devil—the very one who oppose God and his creation that he made in his own image and likeness that would be us the human race man and female.

TEMPTATION: The act of tempting or the state of being tempted specially to do evil. Temptation is a terrible thing when it is against God's Will that is temptation. Truly, there are all kinds of temptations I may say— but let me make it clear what kind of temptation that God is against there is temptation that god is not against such as—you see a good dish of food and your flesh is telling you to go for it. Also, an example is a person will make the statement that, that dish is so tempting well with moderation in place.

Well as for me I like a good chocolate milkshake and they can be so tempting to me at time, but I also drive for a Motor Coach for a living and if I touch that milkshake that was so tempting and good— so soon as I started to drive down the Highway on my journey, well it is my fault, my stomach will start to tumbling and I know this— but it was tempting. It is not a temptation that is harmful to the soul, it just an embarrassing situation for me with a busload of people and when I have to tell them I have to stop— oops my bad, just because my temptation for a milkshake and me driving these two just don't mix for me and I know this but I was tempted and I got a milkshake and I drank the whole thing until I heard the sound from the straw and sometimes that sound is so disappointing because it was so good and it was all gone man it was good too. But the temptation that is harmful to the soul of mankind is anything that God. God has commanded mankind meaning, man and woman, not to do and you do it because it is so tempting to the fleshly desire in which this kind of temptation is always brought to you by the devil because He wants you to disobey God and that disobedience is damaging to the soul.

JAMES 1: 14-15–But every man is tempted, when he is drawn away of his own lust and entice. Then when lust hath conceive, (meaning it is in your mind and you are convinced by that temptation just to do it or commit the act whatever it is —-then it is conceived — just as Eve was tempted.)—it bringeth forth sin: and sin, when it is finished, bringeth forth death.

And that's what happen to Eve. We see it is all in the volume of the book the bible and I am striving to give enough volume of scripture in this book that there are tons of proof so to speak— that God is against Mrs. Clinton running for president of the United

States of America or any other woman trying to run for this office as a president. Temptation have ruined a lot of people lives and organization and marriages family members and so many more etc.

—VERSE—12—Blessed is the man that endureth temptation: for when he is tried, he shall receive the crown of life.

When Eve disobey God by the temptation of the serpent to touch the forbidden tree, she then lost her crown of life and death began to work immediately all because of temptation, Eve will then be second to the man her husband in whom she once was equal with— whom at one time they walk side by side and now this curse that God put on her and every other woman that should be born is also under this same curse that eve is.

If you want to be one with the man women walk together in God's Words and be one in righteousness. This book that I am writing is not the bible but is only a book written by the inspiration of God's Spirit in what He has taught me out of the Bible and about His Word and through scripture and by His Spirit that giveth me the understanding of His Words that is written in the Holy Bible I don't proclaim to be a great author or a good writer I just want this country to know the truth about what God has to say about the women who want to rule here in America as the president in which God forbid.

God is revealing so much unto me— WOW! is all i can say. About this presidential election of 2016 because of a woman and by His Holy Word in which I read and study a lot and I know I can say some things about His will——concerning the estate of mankind and I know that God will be done in this year of 2016 presidential election because cannot go against his word that is written in the Bread of Life called the Bible concerning the females who want to rule here in a country that has such greatness that comes from God's.

This curse was given to all female by God. Not to rule over the man with such authority that the office of the White House as the president has. Mrs. Clinton wasn't even there at this judgment time, when God past judgement on Adam and Eve, but this judgment that God pass is perpetual until the earth is no more and this Word is still in force today because its God's law is given unto the woman you shall not rule over your husband but the husband shall rule over the wife, which the temptation.

When God look in the future of Eve and all the other woman that should be born. God saw all that the woman will be trying to do through the temptation of the Devil.

That will be against his will concerning the judgment that He has passed onto the women and the years to come.

CHAPTER 27

Father Time

What I would say to all "Women be humble, and you will be blessed". The women can't even plea for mercy on this subject. For God has had His say about a woman having the rule over the man.

TEMPTATION–can be a large subject because it started from the beginning of Adam and Eve in the Garden of Eden that's where it all began, right up until the year of 2016 where temptation has grown from that time throughout the world and the tempter is the adversary, known as the devil. Many have fallen into the temptation of the devil.

Why would God be so concerned with this election? Someone may say? Then I will reply; "Gods Words are being put to the test by man to see if God will appear and protect what He has stated in His Word."

GENESIS 3: 16–Unto the woman he said, I will greatly multiply thy sorrow and thy conception; in sorrow, they shall bring forth children; and thy desire shall be unto thy husband, and he shall rule over thee.

There all so many husbands are being ruled by their wives and there are many wives who do not respect their husband as being the man of the house. HOW? — wherein he the man of the house might not hold a job. job or not —or just maybe the wife is the breadwinner of the house and she might just make this statement to her husband, you know I am making the most money so I am going to call the shots around this house well let me say something about that statement that exactly what got Eve in trouble with God and now all the woman of the world and the United States are put under the man and God put it that way, that men and woman might fear Him. Therefore, I say that God is concerned and will involve Himself in this year's election and have the right votes to be for Mr. Trump and at the right time to. Mrs. Clinton will lose this election because God have to protect His Word that all might know that His Word is truth and it will stand forever, and I will repeat this saying and make so much noise about these saying that I am repeating which some of these scripture has been repeated over a 25 or more times that people have got to take notice that there is something about this book and what the writer has to say about God's Word— I WANT TO DRAW ATTENTION TO THE FACTS OF GOD—that there got to be something about what I am saying. AMEN! I hope that when this election is all over that somebody besides me that other than believe and know God like I do which there are some whom I know that will makes the same stand that I am making about the woman being in that much power. God will not allow it.

A spokesman who is an American campaign strategist specialist in politic made this statement that no candidate that has ran for president has ever made it to be president being 10 pts. down. Well, let me make this statement, God is at His best when the odds are against it. The one God that is for will come through for Mr. Trump because he is the man God has chosen to be president for this turn for president of the year of 2016.

God is good at what he does and that working a miracle when things look so bad for Mr. Trump. I know what God's Word says so I must hold on to God's Word. It's because this Word is what I am involved in and that all these Words are found in The KING JAMES BIBLE dated 1611. I a m so proud to live by it and take it for my daily bread it keeps me living spiritually, that I am crying out and writing about this election. Beware and I trust that this book will be display at God's proper timing since August 3, 2016—I've been writing about God's Words and that His Will might be known throughout this world and for the years to come that some of the political party by some miracle get a chance to read this book and about God will concerning who is accepted by God to run for the office as a president of the U. S.A. and that they may make note and realize that God does not except a woman to run for president in this country the United States of America.]AN EXAMP-LE]— I may say, and I just can't say this enough, because that what this book is all about. The woman that have been rejected by God and why, for this certain position. it is all about obedience and the power. I stated early in this book that this book has potential.

In this book there is so much inspirational of thoughts of God's Words being written down on paper and being put into a book format with the wisdom that God has reveal unto me through his word about this presidential race and the knowledge that God has open my mind to and have given me an understanding with such great revelation about something concerning this election. When people are subject unto the higher power which I am writing about, which is the higher power above all. Being subject then God doesn't mind sharing some things with you at time I just cannot write this whole book just on ground surface there are time when God will reveal deep thoughts to my mind that will take me beneath the surface where the deep thing of God is because this presidential race is just too serious to take lightly. Such as I will keep you in suspense/as gods/wisdom first/God knew us before we was born/Satan chose the best among the cattle who was clever /cunning-to deceive Eve].

ROMANS 13: 1 -2 —Let every soul be subject unto the higher powers, for there is no power but of GOD:

Know that the word power is showing and teaching me that there people that are in power that I as a man must be subject to. If Mrs. Clinton could be president of this country, then her husband and her choice for vice president and every other man and woman and I will have to be subject unto her that what this verse 1 is saying. Therefore, if God will allow a woman to become in power as a president of this country the United States of America, loaded with power, then GENESIS 3:16 will be a contradiction to what apostle Paul is writing here.

Since God do not contradict Himself nor in His word, so I can rest my case and pleading on this verse alone that God will not allow a woman to be president of the 2016 election for president. The powers that be are ordained of God. [can we understand that] verse 2: Whosoever, therefore, resisteth the power, resisteth the ordinance of GOD and they that resist shall receive to themselves damnation.

And on this scripture alone I can rest my case and say that God knoweth how to deliver the godly out of temptation.

October 19, 2016–On the third and last debate, something happen that caught my attention and cause me to ponder on what was Mr. Trump replied was when he was ask this question—– "WILL HE, MR. TRUMP, ACKNOWLEDGE MRS. CLINTON IF SHE WAS THE WINNER OF 2016 ELECTION?" And his statement was "I WILL KEEP YOU IN SUSPENSE" O WOW! I see God is in control of this election.

Now that was an upset statement to many, that Mr. Trump gave unto them—and they say it was unconstitutional— (in other words they are saying to Mr. Trump you are authorize under our constitution to acknowledge her as a winner, because of the constitution of our country is which we as American go by)—for you not to accept or acknowledge the winner of your opponent if she, Mrs. Clinton is declared the winner of the 2016 election.

God almighty will reveal unto me as why He wouldn't allow Mr. Trump to acknowledge her as the winner—and I then understood why He couldn't give them the answer that they were looking for because God had to step in and bridle his tongue for a moment and lock up his thoughts. For a moment I may say — and Mr. Trump gave them an answer that God wanted Him to give. The only thing He could say was I will keep you in suspense because God was not going to allow Mr. Trump to acknowledge something that is totally against His Word because it is unconstitutional to God for a woman to be in that much power.

Can we see the hand of God working? Because it is not according to His Word and God will not let a woman to succeed to the White House as president and it will not come to pass because It is just unconstitutional to God. May I also say, that God IS very angry with the Democratic Party and its voter at this moment for putting a woman in the position to be a president of America. God will not allow Mr. Trump to acknowledge Mrs. Clinton as and victor because God has chosen the man Mr. Trump for the position of being president according to his word.

Why would Mr. Trump acknowledge her as a winner? You see God touches the minds of man and control his thoughts. God is totally against a woman being in that much power and God Almighty, the God of Abraham, Isaac and Jacob and so of us who are born of the spirit of God through the teaching of Jesus the Christ.

WHO IS THE CALL? I see nothing but the action of God here and more action will be taken until November-8, 2016, I will see God's Words being manifested unto many that they, and the world might understand that God ruleth in the kingdom of men, and He knoweth how to deliver the godly out of temptation.

You know, I know that the woman is unique, and they can do some good things. It all threw the Bible about the good that some of the women has done even unto our time of the year of 2016—good thing has been done by the woman; but God does not want a woman to be in that much power over the man, and especially as president of the United States of America, this country as of the moment has a clout with God. This country, America, has a gleam about itself that attracts people of all nationality of people flock here like a herd of sheep going to a pasture with such green grass and a stream of water running through the field where they can feast and feed and take a cool drink of water from that stream and then lay down for a peaceful rest, that's America.

COMMANDMENTS: God commands us to keep his commandments so that he can bless us, but somehow the commandment that says a woman should not rule over the man has been overlooking been disobeyed by many or erase out of somebody mind or they haven't been taught of this commandment. — Someone might say where are you getting this stuff from. Well out of the Bible it's calls Godly wisdom that comes from above.

PROVERBS 3:5 – Trust in the LORD with all thine heart; and lean not unto your own understanding. My son forgets not my law; but let thine heart keep my commandments.

1JOHN 5:3–For this is the love of God, that we keep his commandments: and his commandments are not grievous.

Where is the women informer about the higher powers? How far will God allow the female to go in the higher powers of this world? Well I must say that woman has obtained some powerful position in this world. All but one, and I know that they want it and they want it bad. They want to be president of the United States of America in which they have persuaded some men, and women that we need to have a woman president in the United States of America to complete our women's mission.

To prove our point the woman, have a mission to complete we want the big house in this country. As a woman our mission is to attain that office as the first woman to be president of the United States of America in the year of 2016 that our mission and God knows this and by his inspiration, I know this the higher powers.

They, the women, want all the powers that the united states have to offer so that they can say that they the women have been striving for this position for years, since God took it away from Eve, the women, have got one more mission to accomplish and that is the ultimate power of the kings of this world and the power that goes with it to be the ruler of this country. The power that goes with it like a nice suit with everything that come with it to complete the suit—the blouse, the dress, the stockings, the hat, and the women shoes, well that explain the completion of a woman suited apparel.

Now and days, the women suits are shirts, pants, some neck tie, men shoes, and men sock. They are dressing up like men just as God saw it. You see, God is God all by Himself and He saw all of this and more than the woman would be doing to displease Him and he past judgment and put laws and commandment in place that we are compel to obey but I must say to all women; you might put on the men apparels or clothes, but you are still a women in disguise as a man and you are still weak as the bible stated.you just Made all up to look like a man but you are still a woman. You look like a woman, smell like a woman and you walk, and you talk like a woman. Isn't that something you woman ought to be proud of the beauty that God has given and what you have as a female?

When God saw through the end of time and saw the women were going to be changing so he put a limitation on the female and drop her beneath the man. Meaning, now the woman is to be subject unto her husband and she is not to be ruling over him. Had the prophet's priest and minister and the older men and women to address the changes that were going to happen by giving them the commandment to obey. This is a divine rule, a rule to be observed as strictly as one of the ten commandments.

So, I hope I have enlightened someone about the higher power that is given unto us from the Holy scripture from the Bible that the women are forbidden to strive to obtain that position; the highest power in the world as president of the United States of America. It is not in the plan of God for women to rule there because God ruleth in the kingdom of men and the White House is his.

CHAPTER 28

Trouble In The Western Country

I must inform everybody that trouble is coming to the west; the United States, I have seen too many signs in the skies. The skies can tell you to think about the future, but you got to know what you are looking at when the sign appears in the clouds and I have seen in the cloud signs that tell me that the United States will have lots of trouble coming its way. We need a strong man for president because a lot is coming our way American people.

Is the United States really united or divided?

There will be a lot of division in the west. O yes, the cloud has spoken, and they don't lie because it is God who has created the clouds that are above us and the skies but the man that God has chosen for the president of this country will be God's choice, and God's choice was a novice named Mr. Donald J. Trump who has no experience as a president but he is the one that God wants to be the leader of this country because He got a point to prove to this old world and I just can't depend on man or woman to do the right thing in his sight because some men and women are trying to put a women in that spot as president with a lot of persuasion of many.

O, but my God is awesome in defeating the many what he God would call the wicked (evil or morally wrong) O yes again, I may say– it is just wrong for people trying to put Mrs. Clinton in the office as president in God Almighty sight and He will defeat the Democratic Party because He is very displease with them at this time.

BLOWING THE TRUMPET TO GIVE HEED WARNING OF A DISTINCT SOUND: O yes, I going to blow the horn by writing about this election whom God is totally against. One of the candidates, the woman, that has been chosen to defeat the Republican Party nominee, Mr. Trump but I say God has chosen this man I am convinced of its day by day as I see God revealing. If Mr. Trump only knew what I know —if he come to realize, that if he has made it this far standing in the line up to be president of America that its God that has brought him this far —if he only knew that there are righteous people out there, as well as others that are praying for his victory, because we know God will be done on November 8th 2016. Once again, I must say I don't know all that God will allow this man Mr. Trump to do, but my main concern is that the Word of God will stand and the woman of the Democratic Party whom they have put in that position to defeat the Republican nominee Mr. Trump. She will lose the race for the White House because God's Word stands in jeopardy of and by foolish men and women who seem to unlearn about the will of God concerning the women who want to run for the oval office as President of the United States.

Everything that I am writing about is in the Bible it is all there written down in so many places, in biblical scripture but it seems as though somebody feel as though they just don't care what the Bible said, well the horn is being blown that someone may know and come to understand that God's Words will stand, and God himself will defend his Word, and what it has stated. WOMAN SHALL NOT RULE OVER THE MAN.

GOD IS NOT SLACK CONCERNING HIS PROMISE: People sometime think that they can do anything that they want in this world especially when it comes to government worker. Ruler kings as supreme or governor these people who oversee these offices they are responsible for change of the laws and ordinances as we see today in the year of 2016. How those laws are being changed and we as the people of God who obey his commandments are subject to these ordinances that some of the Congress and Senators and Governor are changing.

1PETER 2:13–Submit yourselves to every ordinance of man for the Lord's sake: whether it be to the king, as supreme;

We see again scripture writing about proof of what we as godly people have to do to be in obedience to God Word. Now we see what that kind of storm that is heading our way. Do you think that God is going to be slacking on his promise? What is heading our way? This country wants history to be made and it is in the making, it is in the stove cooking waiting to be done. They are trying to make history by putting a woman in office as president. Let's just say that this making that's in the oven (that I call history) waiting to be done or cook so that they can give or feed this history for the first time unto the American people a woman as president for the first time. I will have to say that we as the Holy and godly people that lives here in America with be subject unto her, because she has become supreme over all the American people as a king— or president.

THE MEAL: The word of God says in the 13 verse of PETER— Submit yourselves to every ordinance of man.

So let's just say, for an example, that Mrs. Clinton has been in this oven cooking for a long time now— waiting to be done because any meal that is being cook in an oven take time to cook and be done so that it can be fed to the guest, so the Democrats are saying to us now that this meal is done and ready to be served or given unto the American people now. Do you get the picture? God knew what was in that oven cooking many years ago

GOD WORD SAYS; man shall rule over the world.

But the men and women of this country have changed the laws and ordinance that God has established from the beginning that are still in effect as of today by God. They have gotten too soft and allow the women to move in and be in rulership in which God speaks against in the churches and as president of a country.

GOD IS NOT SLACK CONCERNING HIS PROMISE: If Mrs. Clinton was to become president believes me laws and ordinances are going to be change and these changes will be against the godly people who live here in America.

Because it's already being set up in motion by some of the democratic party and this is why I say that God knoweth how to deliver the godly out of temptation of this kind of rulership by whom if it were allowed to be. Then it will be a violation against God first, and then toward the godly people who serve Him, and God will not allow his people to be in subject to a woman that way as president.

This is nothing new. It's all written at the beginning of the Bible starting with Adam and Eve. Holiness must not be stopped or bound in this country if this country did not have holy people here, could you just imagine what this country will be like, just do a study on the country that has turned their backs on God and worship and serve other gods and idols.

Stand with God may I say, and you will be blessed — turn from God and you will be a curse that's just fact. Holiness must continue; holiness must be preached; holiness must be taught, and holiness must be practiced and live every day that God might spare us from whatever is trying to come our way.

I remember 9-11. That brought many American to a state of mind to enter in prayer to God. So much pain that was caused on that day that it causes our government, senators, congressmen, governors etc. to kneel on the Nation Capitol steps to pray.

1PETER 15-But as he which hath called you is holy, so be ye holy in all manner of conversation- [Prayer is a holy conversation] Because it is written it is written, BE YE HOLY; FOR I AM HOLY.

I have written somebody got to stand in the gap and pray a prayer that God will hear so I the writer know that God will hear this godly cry, deliver us Lord from this temptation of a woman being president of this country and so I know that God will stand in defense of His gospel. So likewise, I am writing for the defense of the gospel of God. That the world may understand that God is not slack concerning His promise and one of those promises is that the woman will not obtain the power that they are seeking for as president of the United States of America, and the woman's desire. GOD HAS SAID—IT SHALL BE UNTO YOUR HUSBAND, is one of God's promises.

THE LORD'S PRAYER: Praying is a good thing at all time, the whole world or I made say most people are praying for something or another even the presidential nominee is praying to God for that special edge that they need to win this election of 2016. Both Republican and Democrat and a lot of the voter are praying for their candidate to win. Churches of all denomination are praying.

But that just what most people do is pray when they want something that they think is out of their reach— they will step in to a zone of holiness and began to ask God and Jesus for stuff. Yes, stuff that their heart's desire. I see people praying at ball game, for jobs; for homes; for cars; for husband; for wife; for their children. I have witnessed this happening— people praying of all nationalities of race color or creed praying for something even the richest person on God's earth who think they don't need God prays at one time or another for something.

1 THESSALONIANS 5:17— PRAY WITHOUT CEASING.

Those are God's Words teaching all mankind both man women and children do not hesitate to pray.

Why? So that God may hear you cry.

ST. LUKE 18:1–AND HE [JESUS] SPAKE A PARABLE UNTO THEM TO THIS END, THAT MEN OUGHT ALWAYS TO PRAY, AND NOT FAINT;

You see it is in the Bible to pray. We are asking the Holiest (God) for help (PRAYER). I pray all the time mostly all throughout the day prayer and supplication is made for something mostly when I and traveling and when I reach my destination and when I get into my room at the hotel what I usually do first is get on my knees and began to thank GOD for the safe journey and the trip—[prayer]— moving the scene and unseen danger out of my way and giving me a safe journey—[PRAYER—A solemn request for help.

People will get serious when they desire something that they really want, or expression of thanks addressed to God or an act of worship. At one time or another people will step into that of the Holiest and pray (Conversation with God) even when the disciple notice that Jesus will go in a distance from them and pray. They were curious about somethings and that was, just what He was talking to God about.

So when Jesus had finished praying —when He drew close to them they ask him this question master teach us to pray said Jesus said in St. Matthew 6:9–10–After this matter, therefore, pray ye: Our Father (his Father your Father my father)— which art in heaven, Hallowed (TO MAKE HOLY SET APART, SANCTIFY, TO CONSECRATE OR SACRED)—-be thy name. Thy kingdom come, thy will be [in]—-earth— (JESUS SAID in the earth and— not on the earth—— -there is a big difference in the two in—and on—ON)

God will have already been done on the earth when God created it. He wants His Will to be done in this Earthen vessel called mankind [obedience to his word]. So, Jesus is not concern what on the earth, but his main concern is that in the man mind or his heart. So, Christ Jesus said in earth because He wants His Will to be performed in this earthen vessel that men women boys and girls might be obedience to the Will of God.

As it is in heaven means–what in heaven or what's going on in heaven. Well as I understand that God wants us to practice the life that is going on in heaven as I speak[live]

Holy— be and live holy in this earthy body that you have that belong to God—as it is in heaven—cont. —ver. 11

Give us this day our daily bread means that not the bread or food we eat off the table. It is the Word of God; that is the bread that will cause you to live forever. The spiritual food that spiritual food will give you an understanding that God that He does not except a woman as president of this country. Now, what Jesus was saying is that the daily bread that the Lord feed us – thy Word. Because of it, the food for the soul, -if we are spiritually feed then we will be spiritually led if we not spiritually fed we will become spiritually dead. No spiritual understanding of the Will of God—Dead!–And forgive us our debts, as we forgive our debtors. And lead us not into temptation but deliver us from evil: For thine is the kingdom and the power, and the glory, forever. AMEN.

Yes, I say this prayer often even in the month of October 2016. I am saying this prayer that God has given me that He might come down and deliver us from this temptation that's trying to come our way Lord there are some people in this country that are trying to make history. Lord, but Lord, I must say that this thing they trying to do, will put your people in somewhat of abide and I am in that zone of the Holiest by praying and I must pray (praying) because someone might not understand you lord as I do because I know that a woman shouldn't be president of this country but there are so many out their Lord that might not understand this year presidential race for the White House. AMEN.

There are praying right now and saying; "Lord do not let Mr. Trump be our next president is just what a lot of Christians whom understanding is darken and they can't see afar off, and they are praying for Mrs. Clinton to be the next president" My understanding is according to the Word of God and the Will of God. So, therefore prayer is made by the godly people who live in America that understand this situation of this year presidential race of 2016.

That God will deliver the godly out of temptation of a woman being president of the United States of America. That's just will be totally against what we are taught as saints who live in America.

As I have said from the beginning on August 3, 2016 as the Lord inspire me to write about this election because this election is totally different from any other presidential election we have ever had in this country because it is the first woman. That has made it a presidential candidate for the Democratic Party to be, and that itself is history that has been made for the woman and yes that's history that is being made and it will be written down in the history books but I must say so boldly with a period, that as far as God will allow you women to go.

You women will not be able to get to the next step. A runner. That's all just a runner for president but you as women will never be able to obtain that prize as president and I will stand on God's promises because they never fail that promise is written in the Bible which is the Word of God.

JAMES 5:16 – The effectual prayers of a righteous man availed much— and there are so many righteous people who do not understand that a woman shouldn't be in that much power over the man. I do not know why they can't see this but there are some who just don't understand and that is a dangerous thing if I am righteous and you are righteous, we ought to speak the same thing but if one of us faith and spiritual understanding is not on the same level then you might be hoping for a woman president who I am against because of what God's Word has taught me but because of who Mr. Trump is you might be voting for Mrs. Clinton and that is a dangerous thing.

It is a fearful thing to fall into the hands of the living God so be careful and choose wisely.

Hebrews 10:31- It is a fearful thing to fall into the hands of the living God.

Because God has past judgement on the female race from the beginning of time with Adam and Eve and righteous people should understand this a woman President is a no-no in God's eyesight.

CHAPTER 29

The Novice

Aperson new to or inexperienced in a field or situation——now some may say, why in the world has Donald Trump put his name in the ballot to run for president of the united states of America. He doesn't even have knowledge or experience, in that field. He's not a politician. He's just a businessman. He knows nothing about running this country as president. I, myself is saying that Mr. Trump doesn't even know, that God has got plans for him and this one thing that I do know is that God has touched this man Mr. Trump's mind in a very special way. To run. I know that God has got an agenda. The underlying intention or motive of a person or group.

God has got something in mind when He touched this man's mind. The "NOVICE" is what I call him. Mr. Trump run for president. Strange as it may seem to believe it or not, this man is going to win this -1 Corinthians 1: 26 thru 29—for you see you calling,brethren ,how that not to many wise men after the flesh, not many mighty,not many noble,are called -27-But God has chosen the foolish things of this world to confound the things which are mighty;-28-And the base things of the world,and the things which are despised,hath God chosen,yea, and things which are not,to bring to nought things that are;]—these scripture describe MR.TRUMP IN A SENSE,from God's prospective that he has chosen to be the wise and to confound the mighty. He will resurrect and win because God has got a plan for the world to witness. God is going to use a novice to win this race just to prove it to the world that he does not want a woman in that office as president. I know at a time even Mr. Trump himself scratches his head and say, "What are you doing Trump?" But God is going to take a novice against 30 years of experience in the political world and put her to shame–just watch and see.

Sometimes men don't even understand their own way, about, or what they are doing or the direction that they are taking, but God does.

PROVERBS 20: 24–Man's going is of the Lord; how can a man understand his own way.

So, God has chosen this man (the Novice) to run for president and Mrs. Clinton will lose this race because God knoweth how to deliver the godly out of temptation of a woman being president over us as the righteous people who reside in this country. If Mrs. Clinton was to become president this is what we as saint would be subject to her. She would be over us men. She would have the dominion over our body. She has plans that are not good for the godly when a person becomes president we as people of that country are subject unto them and their laws that they will make.

NEHEMIAH 9; 37- 38 – And it yielded much increase unto the king whom thou hast set over us because of our sins:

They have dominion over our bodies, you see that—over our bodies—over our cattle— what we got or —at their pleasure we are in great distress—and therefore God is going to make an example out of this presidential race. By taking a novice to win over a powerhouse in the political arena. The adversary is sure trying to prove God's Words wrong, and when the victory is won by Mr. Trump, people will be very upset because of the outcome.

With just few days left until election time — the Democrats are smiling now because it looks good for them to still now—Throughout the years I learn something about this God, THE GREAT I AM. He doesn't come when you want Him to, but He's always on time just to put to shame the ones who are opposing Him.

I know as I am writing that people will be in question and saying how in the world has this happen. A novice come alone and jump in this presidential race and survive through the stormy weather of the debates and is chosen by the Republican party to represent them as the next president of the United States of America all I can say, it is the handy Work of God.

October 22, 2016–with just 18 days left and Mrs. Clinton seem to be in a joyful state of mind once again, right now because things are looking in her favor once again and she is so happy right now once again, at this time that she is enjoying is sure going to come to naught. This only continue to prove to God just how many people just don't understand His Will.

This also proves how many people who really goes to church and is giving no kind of understanding of God and when you ask them what you learn today in a church they will say O he preach-yes but what did you learn and they will continue to say O he preach so other words they haven't learned nothing. How many preachers out there really just don't know God? Only if they are voting for Mrs. Clinton and they don't have the slightest idea that they themselves are competing against God. I do know that the race will be won by the man—and the smile will be gone for the Democratic voter because the quite God whom people think is asleep will show up for the poll on November the 8th to cast his vote. O yes—by touching certain people's minds and changing people minds toward the Republican Party.

PSALMS 37:39-40–But the salvation of the righteous is of the Lord: He is their strength in the time of trouble. And the Lord shall help them and deliver them: he shall deliver them from the wicked and save them because they trust in him.

GREAT IN EXPERIENCE: Mrs. Clinton does have the experience to be a president and she been very close to that office at one time as the first lady with her husband Bill Clinton who was president in the year of 1992 and she does know some things about the white house and she sure got the experience, in the political field of the political world but with all that experience that she has it doesn't mount anything when disobedience is being done toward Gpd, and also, we can't forget about the Word of God and what it said.

And it is all in the volume of scripture that has come from the King James bible dated 1611. I been compiling much scripture in this book that I am writing as of right now out of the King James Bible since 8-3-2016 until now -10-23-2016. Just to make a point and to prove that God will appear and the experience vs. obedience. The obedience will win (obeying God's Word) and it is what my God recognize at all time-obedience, and not your experience in this case.

If you disobey God, it is against you and you will lose.

FAITHFULNESS: GOD is always faithful. His faithfulness is renewed every morning. Lamentation 3:23 — They are new every morning: great is thy faithfulness, the sun shines and rise every morning.

His faithfulness girds us every day with strength to do his will and his word is also found to be faithful and true at all time if God said something, then you can count it to be true and faithful that it will stand —-steadfast-long time or always there—-regardless of what or who. The reason why the word faithful is brought up because God's Word is faithful and true because God's Word say that the woman shouldn't be ruling over the men. Although Mrs. Clinton is looking good in the polls right now, that doesn't mean anything to God. Maybe it looks good to people, but faithfulness is what I know that God is very good at and He is very faithful when coming to His Word that is written down in the book of life the Bible — remember—steadfast— remember—long time.

DEUTERONOMY 7:9 — Know therefore that the Lord your God, He is God, the faithful God, —

And in this year on November 8, 2016, many will be able to see God's faithfulness come to pass in their lifetime. and mercy with them that love him and keep his commandments to thousands of generations.

I don't have to worry about the polls, and what they are looking like because when you obey the Word of God and His teaching and when we understand that His Word and covenant stand faithful and then we know that God will be faithful in this election and bless us with the deliverance from a woman being over the godly as a president of this country.

Because those who are not godly do not seem to care who is president male or female they just want to be of making history by voting for the wrong candidate in God eyesight and when the Democratic voter has lost, that will be history that you as part of the one who went against all that God was against. They just want to make history, so they can say I was part of that history-making, the proof of this statement is in the pudding I may say—faithfulness.

God will show the godly mercy because we love him and his covenant. I know that the people of this world have tended to go with the wind and to go with the flow— they the people may also say it is the time that we are living in so to speak— whatever the moment is, they go with it because they don't have any gravity in their life to hold them firm to what God has said all about this matter, concerning woman running for president of the united states, somewhere somebody has been misled about God's covenant and commandments.

This covenant started from the beginning of time. EVEN I KNOW THAT. The beginning of time setting the tone, God had to set things in order at the time that disobedience was discovered and because of this act that Eve, and then Adam did, by disobeying the do not touch rule.

TREE IN THE MIDST OF THE GARDEN: God must set the tone and put laws in force, either people are going to please God, or they will not please Him. So, we read in the Bible about men and women disobedience right up unto the year of 2016 people are still fighting and rebelling against God's Word and his covenant, and the laws and the commandments that he has given us, as his creation to obey.

People here in my time are practicing. The thing that God commanded Adam and Eve not to do. I am a witness to these act that are being committee against God. Right today, all I got to do is pick up the newspaper or turn on the news channel I will read or hear about how well Mrs. Clinton is doing in the polls. I am a witness to the fact by the things, what I see and hear of something that God has put in force that she is in disobedience to God's commandment.

Unto the women, striving to overcome the power of God and be dominant over the man that seed that Satan has planted centuries ago is still alive in the woman today and God's Word is still very much alive because of that seed —-and people are still being disrespectful to God. This displeases Him, and He put punishment upon His creation because he created us.

38 or 43 years of experience, I've been serving the Lord and studying his Holy Word which I can say God will prevail in this election and cause Mr. Trump, to be the overcomer, THE VICTOR-YES. I love making this statement —VICTOR! VICTORY! over the woman. As one of the Holy men of the bible made this statement, that the women are the weaker vessel.

1PETER 3:7–Likewise, ye husband, dwell with them according to knowledge; giving honor unto the wife, as the weaker vessel, and as being heirs together of the grace of life; that your prayers be not hindered. -amen—you mean to tell me that somebody is trying to put someone in the white house that is weak.

THE VISITATION OF GOD: An official or formal visit-in in this year of 2016. On November 8, 2016, God will not keep silence. He will draw himself very close to the United States of America because it is election time again and it is time to elect a new president and men and women has gone too far into the desert that they are or seem to be trying God's patience in the things which they are doing to displease him such as trying to put a woman in the White House as president. I must continue once again to make this statement because this is what this book is all about God's Words. The women and men doing something that is totally against God's Will. I can't change people minds, but I can let people know what is true about God and what His Word has said about certain thing such as a woman striving for a very powerful position and I mean a very powerful position that will put her in rulership over a country and the men and women that reside in that country which is none other than America.

God knows I can only tell them what the Bible said about this year election: man vs. woman. I can tell people about this election, but when people don't know God or have an understanding of what His Word is saying, and when they look at them— there polls. I talk country, talk once in a while them their polls. They are convinced by the polls and what the numbers are, and what the media is also saying and not what God's Words are saying.

If people want to see God, just look at this world and its beauty. If people want to hear God speaking, read the Holy Bible and listen to the words you are reading. God often speaks to men and women through His words when we begin to read, and we begin to see with our minds and your mind is your spiritual eyes which will cause you to see things God's way. Because our minds are a spirit just as God is a Spirit.

ST. JOHN 4:24–God is a Spirit: and they that worship him must worship him in spirit and in truth.

God's visitation is near, it is just like a storm that out on the ocean and you know it is moving your way because of the wind and the rain that is on the scene just like the polls are telling a story by the numbers, that Mrs. Clinton is going to win without a doubt they say.

Oh yes, a storm is coming but it will be a storm of disappointment for the Democratic voter, but my God will make his appearance and touch some minds in a mighty way.

And when he makes his visit He will touch the minds of some important folks that matter because time is drawing near and the people that are smiling on the democratic side they are preparing their victory party. May I say with just three days to go and I think that my writing will be done.

I think the victory will be a storm and an upset toward the democratic voter and also among some the Republican Party member who disagrees with there on a body of Republican— man what on earth are you saying you saying? Someone might be saying— O yes, there a discord among the republican people. A derision will be on that day November 8, 2016 because God is good at visiting at the right time and on time and there will be a storm because of the result. They will not be acceptable of the outcome of the polls by many it will be an upset for the Democrats mostly and other beside them.

NOVEMBER 7, 2016 —WASHINGTON, DC.

THE NUMBERS:

LOOK AT THESE DATES, NUMBERS AND THE MONTH

August 3, 2016–97days before election

August—The 8th month- Voting date the 7th- in Washington, DC.

While I was in Washington, DC, 1, 3, &7, AND 8TH

They are some of God's favorite numbers—1s—3s—7s— 8s-

For starter.... GOD IS – 1 and; 3—THE THIRD DAY and Jesus resurrected on the 7TH day.

God rested from His creation of the world—8th day

Jesus was circumcised on the 8th day… and AUGUST 3, 2016 I began to write about the election debates.

JOSHUA 6:1- 27-Like this presidential race first time for a woman to be in a position to be voted as president in the U.S.in which her wall will collapse and fall to the ground-what a storm it will be.

I think it is so strange that I myself have to marvel at the same time about what God does and the time and the dates, that God does these things— all in according to His will—these certain things that are done by God.

The writing of this book I am of a certain— that God took a look into my future one day and then prepare me the novice writer for this time and this day and God knew that I was going to be in the town of Black Mountain NC And just as He did Eve and also Mr. Trump and Mrs. Clinton and God saw what was in the future of the women that should be born up until today's year of 2016 and even to this very day, and also, he looks into Mr. Trump future God took a look.

What so strange to me is this—- God touched my mind and I to started writing this book on August-3-2016, being 97 days before the election day, a novice in writing I may say while I was at the Black Mountains, NC where I was on a bus trip and once I got to this place in Black Mt NC.I had about 4-5 days off and God knew about this ahead of time—for this time and for this purpose I born into this world just little O me the novice writer that is called by God.

I begin to watch the debate of the presidential race, between Mr. Trump and Mrs. Clinton. So, God drew close to me at this time God began to inspire me to write about this presidential race, because he God wanted the world to know the truth, about how He felt about this race for the White House of this year of 2016 presidential race. A woman was involved for the first time in our history as American people of the United States of America and this situation or deed is displeasing to Him because of the fact that men and woman have put a woman in a position that GOD is totally against—striving to make this woman president of the most powerful military country in the world as of now and this is against and His will.

What else is strange———-I am not a writer and neither do I like to write I am a novice at this— just as Mr. Trump also is a novice as being a president of a country for the first time. So, I guess him, and I have something in common, I guess I will learn as I go alone until the election is over but I do know and understand that Mrs. Clinton will not make it this year to the White House as a president because it all written in the Bible, and I understand this, and so does few other Minister also.

But strange as it may seem to believe it or not, God has chosen me to write about this election and I have been writing ever since 8-3-2016. When I have the chance, to write where ever I am. when I am in the motel, at different sports events, at William and Mary college deli at the Williamsburg ,Va. library at home when I can, or whenever I can, but what so strange to me is that God knew my future and he knows my uprising and my down setting, so God knew I was going to be in the nation capital prior, of the election, —[that's god]— when I had no ideal of my future travels or what my dispatch would. O yes, strange as it may seem to believe it or not that where god wanted me to be.

And that where God wanting me to end up so I can be an eyewitness of the event of the election, on hand on site, —I made this statement earlier in this book that I will see this come to pass and not even realizing that God was going to put me right here in the nation capital on election day—[prophecy]— and I feel so special that He has chosen me, Mr. Christopher Smith SR., just and country man born on a dairy farm, a retiree of being a truck driver, who also is a motor coach operator as of now, and when I found out that I would be dispatch to Washington on a 4 day tour of Washington, Dc which will put me in Washington, Dc. at the time that Mr. Donald trump and Mike Pence will be pronounce the winner of the 2016 presidential election—and I was so amaze and come to realize that I was in one of God plan, and truly he[God] has revealed something to me concerning the woman position in this world, what he will allow and certainly what he won't allow, and that, is a woman being in that much power as a commanding chief of our military and as president of America. God forbids! all because of what Eve had done in the Garden of Eden, partaking of the forbidden tree, and this act of disobedience displease God.

And it's just so strange that my travel from the Black Mountains on August 3, 2016, TO Washington,DC ON November,7th 2016 and not knowing my future dispatching.

CHAPTER 30

God Ways Are Perfect

PSALMS 18:30–As for God, his way is perfect: The Word of the Lord is tried; he is a buckler to all those that trust in him

PSALMS 12:6-7–The words of the Lord are pure words: as silver tried in a furnace of earth purified seven times. Thou shall keep them.

O Lord, thou shall preserve them from this generation forever. Everything that I am inspired by God to write is the words found in the bible from the King James Bible dated 1611. That are written down in this book are still active as of today 11—7—2016— and it is still is in force –active.

THE truth of God will be marching on because somebody will pick up the staff and continue the journey of holiness, of daily and godly living every day from day to day of God's Words and its teaching because God has got people everywhere all over this world.

The truth is being told and God has chosen me to be part of this year election to telling the truth and writing about His truth that is written in the Book of Life [the Holy Bible]. That his truth may continue to march on concerning the woman that the Democrats have chosen to defeat the Republican nominee Mr. Trump by attempting to put a woman in the White House as president but God's truth will be marching on November 8th 2016 and just maybe somebody will come to understand that God is against the women in that kind opposition and with the power that it hold.

I mentioned earlier in this book that this book that God has inspired me to write has potential. Qualities or abilities that may be developed and lead to future success or usefulness. This book is full of energy that come from God's wisdom and this book is good for future reference about the female that wants to run for president in the United States of America which is known for its power and the strength of its military, that is granted to us, and it all come from God. AMEN.

You got to cherish the word of God because it will give us life and life more abundantly if you cherish God word like choice diamond—- or something that you value very much—that it is so precious to you.

The word of God is also precious it can guide you when your days seem so dark and you just don't know which way to turn at times, even in this year election it will guide you, when you just don't understand some things about the candidates and just who to choose, this is what King David said when he was in a certain situation.

PSALMS 119: 105–Thy WORD is a lamp unto my feet, and a light unto my path

King David also made this statement in PSALM 119:104– Through thy precepts I get understanding; therefore, I hate every false way. To vote for the woman candidate for president of the United States of America, is a false way to according to God's Words. So, I have taken the God's Way and not the man's way because God's way, will always prevail.

DELIVERANCE: I am confident that the Lord will deliver the godly out of temptation of a woman having the dominion over our body as a president

NEHEMIAH 9: 37-38 – AS NEHEMIAH HAS state on one occasion because we as the righteous people who live a godly life according to God Holy Word in which we that are godly honorand live by its day by day in this present world every day not boasting but that just what the godly people do.

Can you just imagine if there weren't any righteous people living in America? What America would be like? it is the righteous people prayer is what God pays attention to did anyone know that. O yes,

God doesn't hear a sinner prayer because most of the time when the sinner prays he or she always want God to grant them blessing and wants.

And they the sinner don't even obey him nor His Word even I know if you are not a policyholder of a certain insurer you can't even call on them to deliver you when you have a mishap because they don't know who you so go ahead and try to call that insurer, and see what will happen if you have an accident, and you call some insurance company and you are not a member and see what response you will get-zero-o-ooooh nothing but if you a member you have the right to make your claim because you are a member, and now let read what the Bible has said about what I have just stated.

ST. JOHN 9:31—Now we know that God heareth not sinners: but if any man be a worshipper of God, and do his will, him he heareth.

That's why it is so important to obey God every day because there might be a time will when you are going to need him if you are living in sin and love sin so much why not call on the devil and see if he will help you. IF that the one you are serving. If this shoe fit calls on him and see what result you will get o- zero—now I hope you have gotten somewhat of an understanding why it is important to live righteously, and godly in this present world because of trouble that can arise occasionally.

Living righteously is like having money in the bank— something you can fall back on when an emergency arises —it behooves us as God creation to live Holy. it is like having money in the godly bank. Have you ever seem a desolate country which is all dry up and look like it is wasting away? God dry a land up for an example for us to realize we need Him.

Now anywhere the present of god is there is life because of his present—with God their power when god smile on a nation it flourishes. Look at America, it's a flourishing country.

I wish that it could stay that way, so we as the righteous people know that God will appear on tomorrow.

PSALMS 119:126–It is time for the thee, LORD, to work: for they[DEMOCRATS]—HAVE MADE VOID THY LAW.

So, this is what the scripture has said about the Democratic Party has made void thy law by trying to vote a woman into a man position which God has to ordain for men only for this job since the beginning of time and women are prohibited. So, GOD will be GOD on tomorrow's voting day, November 8, 2016.

AMERICA: GOD'S BLESSED NATION

THE UNITED STATES is a very special country to God, and his eyes are on this country like his eyes is on a sparrow.

LUKE 12: 6 – 7–As small as a sparrow is God takes care of it, because the fact of the matter is, that the pilgrim-[who was a small group of people]- came to America to practice freedom of religion and this act please God. Because the pilgrim who travels from afar wanted to worship and serve GOD freely this also please God and God hast bless this country to become very prosperous and a powerful nation as well.

THE SEED: When America was established in 1776, it had a purpose and a gold in mind— FREEDOM, and they were willing to fight and die for that freedom just to be free, and that seed of freedom was planted or instill into the minds of the American people from generations to generations and as we see freedom is still fought for today in some form or another.

The ERA- has taken the freedom to a different level they want the right to do whatever the men do, and this action displeases God- where is God reverence-do we disrespect our father and mother of the flesh and their wishes or do we strive to please them accord to that which is right in God eyesight —freedom.

Do you know that 83% of the people who live here in America worship GOD one way or another? And did you know that the United States aide to other country is up to 96%? To help the other country in this world— and 48 billion dollars is given to the aide of some military in other countries around the world, to help them with freedom from there enemy.

This is the love of God. God has blessed this country for the love that they have shown towards Him and to other nation, and with the help that they the American have given to other nation to help to be free—FREEDOM———-and by these acts of kindness that the American people have shown God also has stepped in and cause this country America to be what it is today and a country that believes in freedom.

Shall we, as the American people, jeopardize that. All that we have here by being disobedience to God over this matter because you called it a freedom to put a woman in office at the White House as president? I just can't seem to express this enough why stand we in jeopardy every hour with God do we want our freedom to be dismissed from us. O yes, God can take it all away in just a moment.

I must proclaim the gospel of God on this matter because a sore disobedience is among the American people how can a nation of people be so blinded by a movement just to make history.

the first woman chosen by the Democratic Party just might have a chance to become president in America they believe. Well, now since you have made this stand now God knows who you all are now. With all that noise that you have been making since this election has started and with all such boasting that God will put to naught on November 8, 2016. All of you have been exposed now God know what your stand is.

WHERE DOES AMERICA STAND WITH GOD TODAY? or may I say what God feeling about this country today——-if GOD is for you?

I hope that God is still smiling on us and have not taken His hands-off America because if He ever does Lord have mercy. The enemy will come in like a flood and take hold of all the American freedom and do away it little by little, they have already begun but I hope that God's grace will still abound here. God will have mercy on the godly people who live here. Which I am sure that he will and put a stay on all of Democrats plan whosoever they may be.

When all the ballots are counted, there will be a cry made— some of the rejoicing and a lot of crying for disappointment because their history wasn't made for the woman here in America.

As I am touring my group that is from Florida around Washington DC we are now at the Franklin Delano Roosevelt Memorial and while I was sitting and waiting on my group who is visiting that memorial I began to look across the Tidal Basin at the Thomas Jefferson Memorial statue it is, 19 ft- (5. 8m) tall

And as I was beholding these memorials around the Basil, I began to hear helicopter flying over my head and I thought to myself "These guys are flying from the Pentagon to Camp David At Thurmont, Maryland with the military high-ranking personnel and other, tendering to the U. S. affairs as well as other countries affairs as well"

you see, that's proof of what America is all about standing tall just like the Thomas Jefferson statue and to protect this country and the other that are less fortunate than we are.

God has ordained men for that job from the beginning of the first kings and their men of armor and God has commanded the woman to not put on that which pertaineth unto men. I can take this subject and go in so many directions of its meaning, I just want to simplify this saying of God— Women do not strive for that which God has ordained for men or that which also pertaineth to men only -the ultimate power of this country as president.

On this last day before the election date, I am still writing about the woman that's trying to overcome God's commandment. No doubt will the woman be denied and that mean Mrs. Clinton and all the other woman who is following the same pattern.

May I say one more time because of God chooses men because of their strength that they possess, the woman doesn't hold this strength that God is looking for in —men- and that the strength that God wants for America is very strong in a many of way.

The weakness of the female was proven from the beginning of time with eve and just because the women go to the gym and lift or press all can of weights. Just to try to build their body muscle so that they can say I am just as stronger than you men are. Yes, I can run that office they say at the White House as president of the USA. Maybe they can, without a doubt. I got some good news for all your physical fit, exercising bodybuilding muscle female.

1 TIMOTHY 4:8–For bodily exercise profiteth little: but godliness is profitable unto all things

This is where Eve fail at godliness she wasn't strong enough to reject the Serpent lie having a promise of the life that now is, and of that which is to come. This is a faithful saying and worthy of all acceptation. These things command and teach.

You see why I have taken God's side, because if God said something, it is just truth so may I say out of the 22 women that are in power around the world as prime minister or such. These countries that the woman is in power, does not hold the power that the United States has, that's what concern God— the power—and the American military has power and the commanding chief as well has power —the top— very top. Aren't you glad that we are protected by such power? Well I am. god knows how to deliver the godly out of temptation.

THE TRUTH DAY

PSALMS 118:1–This is the day which the Lord hath made; we will rejoice and be glad in it. Who will rejoice?

I for one will be rejoicing because I believe if God has chosen me the novice to write about this event the 2016 election, then no doubt the Republican is going to win this 2016 election.

Well volume 1 of this book is ending and I think, and I've been here writing for 97 days before the election. When I start on August 3, 2016, at the township of Black Mountain North Carolina. Where I was inspired by God to write all that God must inspire me to, and I have written according to what I have heard and what I as a person have seen and what I am a witness of or to, and thanking the Lord for this day that he the Lord has made truly this has been somewhat of a strange and peculiar journey for me—by not being a writer.

A writer is a person who writes books and stories for a living or article or column for some newspaper as a regular occupation and that not me— which I am not a writer just novice.

CHAPTER 31

The Two Novices

Mr. Donald Trump, Upcoming Us President And Mr. Mark Smith, A Novice Writer.

Novice: A person new to or inexperienced in a field or situation. You see how God does things in one's life and how that God can inspire one to or urge someone to do things according to His Will. Let me note this one thing if someone would have told me that I one day will be writing about a great event such as the 2016 election between the two-running mate. Man: Mr. Trump; Woman: Mrs. Clinton— for the president of the United States of America

I am not a writer, plus it takes some time and it take so long just to complete an article. Well, God is all that I can say, on this matter. God is so amazing that He wants little old me, to write about this president election. Between the man and the woman, in whom He is very displease with the woman, because of the position that she has been chosen for by the Democratic Party to strive for as president of America...

Somehow this seemed to me that this is all a set up by the Democrats just to see what will happen. Somebody may already know that God doesn't except a woman in the USA as a president, but that someone is keeping quiet.

If our gospel is hidden its hid to those that are loss maybe just maybe Mrs. Clinton don't know the facts about God's command that

He has put on the women and of all the women threw out the ages of time even until now.

In whom the God of this world hath blinded the minds of them which belief not, lest the light of the glorious gospel of Christ, who is the image of God, should shine unto them. To give an understanding of a thing-manifest,

The truth of God and His Word is the light to give all men and women and understanding of His Will for us to follow and be obedient to – Today is The National election day and it somewhat quiet day around our nation capital— the weather is great here in Washington DC with a few helicopters about I guess a lot of folks are out at the polls preparing to vote for their candidate.

THE SUN IS SHINNING: On this day November 8th, 2016, the sun is shining bright, like the radiant of God's light to me this is a sign from God that His Word will be shining today for the righteous and the godly people who live here in America. It will be shinning for the Republican Party Today. O yes, what a day of rejoicing it will before the godly people and the Christian and The Republican Party and their supporters. As more military helicopter flying over our head with these important people that they are carrying from one place to the other.

While I am still touring my Floridians group around the memorial in the Korea War Veteran Memorial. World War 2 Memorial, Vietnam Veterans Memorial and the African American Civil War Memorial—over which 209,000 of the U.S. colored troops who serve during the civil war (1861-1865) located in Washington DC. ON Vermont and U-ST NW and the other memorial that I might have left out—Freedom.

THE SPIRIT OF FREEDOM: You see freedom -protection-from our enemies and all these memorials is proof that somebody care and gave their lives for the freedom of all races color or creed that we as American might have freedom and be free.

And this is what we have in this country today—freedom— but some are using this freedom that we have as American in another way, and that is a woman right to run for president of the most powerful country in the world and its military strength and for this deed that they are trying to produce or bring fruitation or to pass. Well let me say this vintage shall and will not come to pass because the sun is shining toward the godly people and the republican today because God truth will be marching on today.

I say thank you Lord for the wisdom and the understanding of your Word so that I want to be in a decision on November 9, 2016, when all the result is in and Mr. Donald Trump is declared the victor of the 2016 president election.

Now, the night of the 8th of November is upon us, my group is visiting the World War 2 memorial and so while I am waiting for them to come back I took time out for myself. So, as I was looking across the lawn toward the Washington monument standing— so tall 555 ft. Dedicated in memory of our first president who also was 6ft tall and so is our president to be. Mr. Trump —6ft. 2—inches— standing tall like the other, and then I was inspire by God to kneel and pray, o yes people protest in our nation capital so why can't I pray, and I was lead to pray the prayer that Jesus taught his disciples.

OUR FATHER- which art in heaven—Hallowed be thy name—Thy kingdom come —They will be done in earth as it is in heaven—give us this day—our daily bread—-And forgive us our debts—as we forgive our debtors— AND LEAD US NOT INTO TEMPTATION, —-BUT DELIVER US FROM EVIL—-FOR THINE IS THE KINGDOM—-AND THE POWER—-AND THE GLORY—-FOREVER——AMEN.

THE NIGHT OF THE ELECTION: One more scripture is given to me, that found in the book of GENESIS 1:26—-And God said Let us make man in our image, after our likeness: and let them have dominion over the fish of the sea,and over all the fowl of the air,and over all the cattle, and over every creeping thing that creepeth upon the earth.

At this time, God was including Eve whom was not created yet, but she was in the plan of being part that dominion, but Eve mess up and God drop her beneath the man Adam, so we learn from this scripture God was including Eve in all of His plan for mankind. Over the fish of the sea, and over the fowl of the air, and over the cattle, and over all the earth, and over every creeping thing that crept upon the earth do we as reader get this or my DAD will say you get the point.

Man was created in God's image. The woman was created in the man's image God said for the men to have the dominion. This saying was giving to man before Eve was created. Man is to have the dominion. God has stated, since this is true. When did the woman get permission from God to have the dominion over the man and everything or where did she get the ideal from?

THESE ARE THE QUESTION THAT SHOULD BE ASKED.

When a woman wants to rule over the man, then the woman got her permission from—Lucifer/ the serpent/Satan/the devil himself and not God.

When Satan uses the Serpent to tempt Eve in the garden of Eden, with that temptation, by saying: "Go ahead and touch that tree Eve, it will change your life"

As she was tempted and did eat of the forbidden tree, this act of disobedience, that was committee on that day and hour that she did partake of, it became a sin, and that sin was against God totally. you see the adversary. She never got permission from the BOSS to eat of that tree or to be a ruler, and to have dominion over man. THAT BOSS IS GOD.

CHAPTER 32

The Announcement

The Announcement Came In The Ballots Has Been Counted And Mr. Donald J. Trump Is The 45Th President Of The United States Of America!

AMEN, AMEN, and AMEN.

God has delivered the godly out that temptation thank you Lord for being a true God. As I've faith in God and believing in your word that you will come through for the godly people I just hope that every man and women, boy and girl that have the opportunity to read this book that was written by the inspiration of God's Spirit and written by my hands will come to believe in thy word that it is nothing but truth.

I THANK YOU, LORD, FOR THE VICTORY THAT YOU LORD HAVE GIVEN TO MR. DONALD TRUMP PRESIDENT OF THE UNITED STATES AND MIKE PENCE VICE PRESIDENT. OVER HIS OPPONENT MRS. HILLARY CLINTON, I JUST HOPE THIS BOOK FINDS ITS WAY INTO TO HER HANDS, THAT SHE MIGHT KNOW AS WELL, THAT GOD RULETH IN THE KINGDOM OF MEN, , AND AS LONG AS THIS COUNTRY AMERICA DONT LOSE ITS FACE VALUE WITH GOD, THIS LAW WILL ALWAYS BE IN EFFECT IN THIS COUNTRY, I WILL ENCOURAGE MRS CLINTON, ITS EVE FAULT. AND THAT LAW WAS ESTABLISH LONG BEFORE YOU WAS BORN.

Well as it has been written —derision-bumfuzzle-has taken its action on this day November 9, 2016 people are upset and confuse. the rioting[rampage] has begun the protester are out in the street saying this is not America [I am a witness to this because I was a couple block away], and he, not my president they are saying.

Well let me say this, other country has women prime minister and president, but America has men for their president. Other countries have a weakness about themselves. That God is not please with it. So, we find that women are ruler there—because these countries do not have the power that America has. It is all about the power folks, the power. God gave men certain power and He created the world and gave man the dominion over it. God's Words has been honored by God and it is protect by God and God's Word.

Do not lie as some me do, so I must conclude this book by saying....

Thank you, Lord God of all flesh, for being a perfect God who hand is not shorten that it cannot save. Just hearing the godly people humble cry saying save us Lord from a woman presiding over us as the president and may I say I hope that this book hasn't offended someone in any way if it has please forgive me because the truth has to be told in some way or another. Now my last writing shall be a prayer for our new president that has been nominated of the year of November 9, 2016 alone with his vice president Mr. Mike Pence.

[the conclusion Prayer for our new president and vice president and their administration that God has given.

NOW LORD GOD ALMIGHTY, YOUR WORD, AND WILL HAS COME TO PASS. YOU HAVE GIVEN THE VICTORY TO Your CHOSEN MEN. I PRAY LORD THAT THESE MEN AND THEIR FAMILY WILL BE PROTECTED FROM DAY TO DAY. THIS WILL BE A LONG JOURNEY FOR THEM, BUT LORD GOD GIVE THESE TWO MEN THE PATIENCE THAT IS NEEDED TO MAKE THIS JOURNEY AND THE TASK THAT YOU HAVE CHOSEN FOR THEM AND PROTECT THEM AS THEY TRAVEL FROM PLACE TO PLACE— FROM THE NORTH, SOUTH, AND EAST TO WEST. BE WITH THEM BOTH FROM DAY TO DAY AND GRANT THEM

WISDOM AND THE KNOWLEDGE TO DO THE JOB THAT THEY HAS BEEN CHOSEN FOR, BECAUSE I KNOW LORD THAT MANY WILL RISE UP AGAINST THEM, BUT LET YOUR PEACE LORD REIGH IN THERE HEARTS AND LET ALL ANIMOSITY BE DISSIPATED OR BE SCATTERED— AWAY –THAT THESE TWO MEN MAY ATTENDED TO THE AFFAIRS OF THIS COUNTRYAS WELL AS THE OTHER.

AND LORD REMEMBER THIS COUNTRY AMERICA, AND ALL OF THE DISAPPOINTED VOTER WHOM CANDIDATE HAS LOSS—REMEMBER THEM ALSO, AND REMEMBER MRS. CLINTON AS WELL, AND HER FAMILY WATCH OVER AND PROTECT THEM AS WELL, AND GIVE THEM UNDERSTANDING OF ALL OF THIS THAT HAS COME TO PASS LORD AND I THANK THE O MIGHTY GOD FOR ALLOWING ME TO BE A PART OF THIS GREAT COUNTRY AMERICA AND ALLOWING ME TO WRITE ABOUT THIS 2016 ELECTION AND REMEMBER US ALL

IN JESUS CHRIST NAME AND THANK YOU LORD FOR NOT BENDING YOUR RULES. AMEN, AMEN AND AMEN

-THE END-

Mark C. Smith

Now why people would people of all color and creed be interested in reading this book? Why Mrs. Clinton didn't win the election? Why women always fail in the United States to become president?

God knoweth how to deliver the godly out of temptation. God's commandment still live on in the year of the 2016 election. This is the truth and what The Bible says about women being in total power of the most powerful country in the world – the United States of America.

CPSIA information can be obtained
at www.ICGtesting.com
Printed in the USA
BVHW092136011118
531917BV00014B/73/P

9 781643 670850